GW00676395

DETERRENT OR DEFENSE

DETERRENT

A Fresh Look at

NEW YORK

B. H. Liddell Hart

OR DEFENSE

the West's Military Position

FREDERICK A. PRAEGER, *Publishers*

*Published in the United States
of America by Frederick A.
Praeger, Inc., of 64 University
Place, New York 3, N. Y.,
U.S.A.*

*Published in Great Britain
by Stevens and Sons Limited
of 11 New Fetter Lane,
in the City of London,
and printed by The Alcuin Press,
Welwyn Garden City, Herts.,
England.*

Library of Congress catalog card number 60-12092

©
B. H. Liddell Hart.
1960

To

Kathleen

in gratitude for all her help

CONTENTS

IV. TACTICAL

V. ALTERNATIVE PROPOSALS

VI. EPILOGUE

PREFACE

THIS book is an endeavour to sum up the strategic situation as it stands today and to bring out its meaning and message. Ten years have passed since I last published a book on current problems of defence, although during the interval I have written numerous articles and memoranda, privately circulated, about various aspects of the subject. In the last two years I have concentrated on a series of special studies into problems which seemed to require re-examination and further exploration, circulating the successive drafts for discussion, and subsequently developing them. I have now woven them into the pattern of this book, along with some of the earlier material that has a continued relevance to the key issues of the present and the future.

In a short book *The Revolution in Warfare*, published soon after the first atomic bombs had been dropped on Japan in 1945, I discussed the implications of nuclear war and pointed out what seemed to me the long-term risks and boomerang effects, strategically and politically, of reliance on nuclear weapons for the enforcement of policy and the preservation of peace. In *The Defence of the West*, published in 1950, I elaborated my conclusions about the consequences, and particularly as to the inherent limitations and drawbacks of dependence on such weapons as a counter to aggression, and as a deterrent. A few weeks after the publication of that book, the Communist invasion of South Korea was launched, and in its course demonstrated the limitations. So did the war in Indo-China.

In 1954 the power of atomic armament was enormously increased by the development of the thermo-nuclear weapon, commonly called the "Hydrogen Bomb". But at the same time such power had ceased to be an American monopoly, while Russia was gaining a lead in the development of long-range missiles, which promised a more effective and less interceptible means of delivering a nuclear attack than aircraft could provide.

The mutual possession of nuclear weapons tends to nullify the value of possessing them. For even a decisive superiority of numbers does not ensure victory, as it has with other weapons, but merely mutual destruction—and there are no degrees of importance in the matter of suicide. (That defining word has to be constantly reiterated because the fact is otherwise so difficult to realise by minds accustomed to think in terms of other weapons, and thus inclined to regard nuclear power as "just another weapon" added to the armoury.) The natural consequence of such nuclear parity is nuclear nullity.

Thus the nuclear deterrent, in which the West has put so much trust, is fading except as a deterrent to its own kind of action. For when its use spells suicide for the user, other forms of aggression may proceed with impunity if they are limited in aim and action. In particular, such a situation offers renewed and increased scope for the surprise coup or sudden pounce that can produce, swiftly and almost bloodlessly, a *fait accompli*.

My book is focused on the problem of "the fading deterrent", and its replacement.

B. H. LIDDELL HART

States House,
Medmenham.
May, 1960

PART ONE

RETROSPECT

1

A RUSSIAN "LOOK" IN 1952

[*This was written at the end of 1952 in answer to a question then put to me as to how the Russians might view the strategic situation, and " what course would you propose if you were Chief of the Russian General Staff? " It helps to show the potential dangers at that time, and the situation as it was before the multiplication of atomic weapons and the production of the H-bomb.*]

" I HAVE spent all my life in trying to guess what was at the other side of the hill." That was one of Wellington's best-known sayings. It aptly defined the primary requirement in generalship, and in statesmanship—to guess what is going on behind the opposing front, and in the opponent's mind. Imagination is as important as information, and all the more where the latter is unreliable. To look at the situation—especially *your* situation—from *his* point of view is the best way of trying to get into his mind.

In confronting the problem that Russia presents today we are labouring under several handicaps that are heavier than any in our past experience.

One is the combination of immense material resources with a fanatical spirit and faith. Their dynamism is dynamite in the world today.

Another handicap is the inscrutable nature of the Russian mind, and the difficulty for Westerners of penetrating into its thought-processes. The Russians' difference from their

3

European neighbours has been multiplied by Marxist indoctrination and by isolation.

A third handicap is lack of reliable information about the situation inside Russia, militarily and politically. Even in 1942–45 when we were her partner in the fight against Hitler, we were far more in the dark about her forces than about the German. While we knew where almost every panzer or infantry division lay, and where they moved, we had only a dim idea of the number of divisions in any Russian army ! It is even dimmer today.

The Allied statesmen and military chiefs have often stated that Russia has 175 divisions in her standing Army. Such a figure sounds impressively precise, but is little better than a guess. It is possible to get a fairly accurate picture of her forces in the occupied and satellite countries, but not of those which lie further back, deep inside Russia. Not only is her security network extremely tight, but her vast space aids concealment. The Iron Curtain is a flimsy screen compared with such depth.

Our information today about Russia is in many ways hazier than ever, and where it is specific is more dubious. So, in trying to gauge her leaders' likely moves, the best guide may be to place ourselves imaginatively in their seats and look at the situation strategically from their point of view. Strategy is a practical matter, and less doctrinaire than political theory, while also less influenced by racial modes of thought. Although the military profession has been the strongest servant of nationalism it has an international way of thinking in its approach to problems.

If I were the Chief of the Russian General Staff I should feel much satisfaction with my " hand of cards " on the military level, and with my Government's on the higher level. I wouldn't like to exchange these hands for those which Russia's Western opponents have to play, on either level.

But I should advise Stalin against risking war in a major way unless sure of solving one problem, and seeing a good chance of solving another. (I might not put the matter quite so bluntly in talking to Stalin, but rather remind him how shrewdly cautious he had always been, and how he had said that he would take care not to repeat Hitler's mistakes.)

" In the first place," I would emphasise, " Russia must make sure that she can annihilate Britain quickly—not so much because of Britain's own power, but because of her key position, just off the continent of Europe, as a base for American counter-attack, particularly with atomic bombs.

" Secondly, we must be able to see a good chance, and effective way, of paralysing counter-action by the U.S.A. for a lengthy period. ' It will not be enough,' I should say, ' to overrun Europe and sweep the Americans out of it, unless we can ensure ample time for them to cool down, in a state of impotence, and come to the conclusion that there is more to lose than to gain by a prolonged and destructive effort to recover their hold on Europe.' "

Having made these two fundamental points, I should amplify them. As Chief of the Russian General Staff, and an objective-minded strategist, I should not be deluded by the Party's post-war propagandist line that Britain had played a negligible part in Hitler's defeat. It would be clear to me that Hitler's first and most fatal mistake was that he had not thought out, nor been prepared for, the problem of conquering Britain after overrunning the Continent. Because he could not cross the English Channel—a super-scale anti-tank ditch that baulked his otherwise decisive panzer forces—he had been impelled to turn East while still entangled in the West, and to strike at Russia without being able to concentrate his full strength for the blow. Thereby he had forfeited the tremendous advantage he enjoyed after the fall of France. Moreover, by failing to subdue Britain, this " island on the

5

edge of the Continent " became both the base of America's bombing forces and the springboard for the liberating invasion of Europe. I should not be likely to overlook this lesson in my own planning.

" Ever since World War II ended in 1945 I've had the General Staff at work on the problem of how to knock out Britain. Indeed, this study began even earlier. For as soon as it appeared that Roosevelt and Churchill were really trying to smash Germany completely, and leave her no forces to act as a defensive barrier, it became obvious that they were opening the way for us in western and southern Europe. How blind they were! So we naturally started to look for a solution of the ' British island ' problem that had baffled Hitler.

" I early came to the conclusion that Russia ought to create the largest possible airborne forces with a view to ' jumping ' over the Channel, and over the heads of the British fleet—as our Navy is even less likely than Hitler's to gain command of the sea. In World War II we had more trained parachutists than any other country, yet lacked adequate air transport to use them effectively. That was not the only reason, however, why we never attempted airborne operations. There was no great call for these once we were on top of the Germans—so it was worth while to keep this card up our sleeve, and lull our next opponents to sleep about the danger of airborne invasion.

" Since Germany's collapse, we have been building up proper airborne divisions, and an air transport fleet, as well as long-range fighters. In World War II we concentrated our air effort mainly on tactical support for the armies, and those types of fighter were not suited for escort missions against distant objectives.

"Of course, I realise that a large airborne force is very vulnerable, and difficult to carry through to its objective in face of even a moderately strong air defence. But there are several cards we can play. The first is to launch our airborne force against England by surprise before war has broken out, so that we can catch the British when they are not mobilised. A week-end would be a good time—they are normally off their guard then, and it would be much easier to produce a paralysing upset. This airborne stroke would be immediately followed by a general advance of our armies in Europe, so that each blow would help the other, and give the enemy all the less chance to recover his balance.

" We were a bit worried last year when the British showed signs of awakening to the danger of a surprise descent from the sky, and began to revive their wartime Home Guard as a precaution—but the British newspapers show that recruiting for this citizen force has been a flop, and I don't think most of their people are taking the danger seriously.

" The British are naturally inclined to look on such an operation from their own point of view, and be governed by their own habit of mind. Their military leaders were usually very cautious in the last war, and particularly careful about ensuring ample supplies. So they probably think that no one would drop a large force at a distance, and into an island, where its maintenance would be precarious. They have not got over the shock of the failure of their own venture at Arnhem. Moreover the British, with their limited manpower and excessive care for their men, may find it hard to imagine that any one would venture to cast a large body of troops into a place where they might be isolated and massacred before our air force could gain such command of the sky and the sea as to make cross-Channel reinforcements possible.

" The British and Americans don't realise that our Russian troops are accustomed to live on very little and carry on for weeks at a time without the supplies that a Western Army deems essential—foraging for themselves in the country where they are fighting. Nor can our enemies really understand that we can be quite ruthless in sacrifice, and that our men don't jib at being sacrificed in ' suicide ' operations. Even if we were to lose one or two airborne corps in such a descent on England that would be a fleabite compared with what we lost in our opening battles against the Germans. We don't mind big initial losses when playing for big stakes.

" Another way of landing a force in England by surprise, and before we had won command of the sea and sky, would be through an undersea invasion—in submarine troop-carriers. We've been working on that problem. But it calls for a very big development, which takes time and carries various complications. In the light of the Russian Navy's limited experience and performance in war compared with the Army I'm not very confident of it having the skill and drive to carry through such a project. So an airborne raid seems the better bet, at any rate in the immediate future.

" However, Stalin may decide against it. He has never been inclined to strike unless very sure of success. The kind of audacious gamble that Hitler loved has never appealed to him. Moreover, its best chance would lie in launching it as a complete surprise when the British are not mobilised—but that would obviously put the onus of aggression on us. For political and psychological reasons it may be wise to ring up the curtain with a land-battle on the Continent, where we can more easily make it appear that our offensive is a retort to an enemy violation of frontiers. Stalin does not think only of ' strategy ', but rather of ' grand strategy '—the higher plane where political and military action are combined.

" If Stalin turns down this ' out of the blue ' stroke against England, there are several other opening uses for our airborne forces in closer combination with a land attack.

" One is to drop them beside the Rhine bridges—in order to capture these intact for the passage of our armies, while

8

cutting off the Allied forces stationed east of the Rhine and blocking the move-up of Allied reinforcements.

"Another is to drop them on Denmark and the south coast of Norway—to capture the outlets from the Baltic for the passage of our submarines.

"We might also drop them on the Alpine passes leading from Austria into Italy, or—further afield—on the passes in Persian Azerbaijan leading into the plains of Iraq. These last two strokes would call for relatively small forces so we might be able even now to execute them without seriously diminishing the strength required for either of the big strokes. The total of our ground forces, too, is much larger than we can effectively employ in western Europe, so we could well provide sufficient divisions to follow up the airborne 'tin-openers' into Italy and the Middle East. The more widely we develop our threats the more confusion and demoralisation we shall cause.

"Given time to continue our air and airborne development, we may be able to carry out both the big strokes simultaneously, and on an adequate scale, as well as the smaller ones.

"If it becomes a matter of choosing between the Rhine crossings and Baltic outlets, I would be inclined to the latter —for it is so important to get our submarines out in full force into the Atlantic to block the ocean supply-routes from America to Europe, and especially to England.

"I'm not counting too much, however, on such a submarine blockade proving decisive—as Hitler and Admiral Doenitz hoped theirs might be. Although in 1945 we captured the latest German submarine designs, which have been a great asset, that is not the same as having a submarine force equal in skill and experience to the German. There's a lot of leeway to make up among the personnel.

"In any case we must solve the problem of knocking out

America's advanced base in Britain, and of doing it at an early stage of the war. How could it be done ? Once we have overrun the western part of the Continent, and occupied the coast, the Russian air force should have a very big superiority over the British and American air strength remaining in the south of England, and we may be able to dominate the Channel sufficiently to push across an invading army. It was only by a narrow margin that Hitler failed to win the 1940 ' Battle of Britain ' in the air—and he wasn't prepared for the problem he tackled. He had not even got the armoured landing craft required to carry his assault troops, whereas we've had plenty of time to build them in quantity.

" If we don't succeed in gaining sufficient mastery of the Channel to get our invading army across in overwhelming strength, there are other cards we should be able to play. One is an atomic bombardment—delivered by our air force or by the guided missiles that we are now developing. Another is a bacteriological bombardment—Britain being an island, there is less risk to us that this might become a boomerang.

" In view of our great advantage in strength for the normal kind of land offensive, we might keep these cards up our sleeve until America plays hers. For there is sure to be much protest, from her allies in Europe who are closer targets, against her starting to ' atomise ' cities if we at first refrain. There is a risk in refraining, but the profit could be greater. So it's a question of launching the bombardment of England after reaching the Belgian and French coast, or of launching it earlier at longer range—as we can do with our new strategic Bomber Force.

" It is vital to us in any war that Britain should be quickly ' eliminated '. The surest way would be to make it uninhabitable—turning it into a desert island. That would also be simpler than trying to convert its people to Communism. We can occupy and repopulate it at leisure, if we choose to do so—though there is much to be said for keeping it merely as a military outpost on the Atlantic coast, occupied purely by a Russian garrison. A scientific strategist should look at problems in a cold-blooded unemotional way. Even the British and Americans did not let their boasted ' humanitarian ' scruples hinder them from devastating Germany regardless of the human consequences. The complete ' elimination ' of opposition is the most effective, perhaps the only effective, way of solving problems finally. The Nazis realised that, though they went about the job in such a secretive and shame-faced way that they bungled it. Coolly logical Marxists should be more effective than sentimentally passionate Nazis —half-baked totalitarians !

" Now that America has taken southern Europe and the Middle East under her wing, as well as western Europe, we have got to reckon that there is much less chance of our being able to achieve local advances anywhere without producing a general war. So if it comes to military action we can no longer contemplate limited objectives—it's all or nothing. That makes it the more necessary on our part to aim at the annihilation of Britain, and to give it priority in our planning.

" If Britain can be annihilated, we shall not have much left in Europe to worry us. The French are still very poorly equipped, thanks to delay in American production and the inefficiency of their own—and that's not likely to raise their morale above the 1940 level! The West Germans are still un-armed, and even if the wrangling over their rearmament eventually ends, it will be at least two years before their pro-posed contribution of twelve divisions is ready. Now that we've mechanised a large part of our Army we should be able to overrun most of the Continent very quickly. The NATO powers have barely twenty divisions in immediate readiness, whereas we have three times as many to form the mechanised spearhead—with plenty more to follow them up,

11

while the NATO reserves are scanty. Should it become necessary, we could smooth our progress with a few atomic bombs, or the threat of them. Even if we were temporarily checked on the fringes, such as mountain-girt Spain or sea-girt North Africa, these don't offer facilities comparable to England as bases for an American counter-offensive. In Africa, too, it should not be difficult to stir up sufficient trouble among the natives to impede the development of American bases until we can invade it. They're already on the boil.

" So there seems a good prospect of keeping the Americans at a distance, and for a time long enough to damp their ardour—if Britain can be liquidated. Our propaganda could help by sounding the note : ' If you send your boys to Europe, you'll never see them again—it's a one-way ticket to Siberian prison-camps.'

" Of course we must expect long-range bombing from the American continent, but there would be a better chance of checking it, or at least curtailing it, than shorter-range bombing from bases in or near Europe. Moreover, there is reason to doubt whether the Americans, with their extremely vulnerable cities, would obstinately carry on a prolonged competition in atomic bombing under such conditions. The more highly developed civilisation has more to lose, and would suffer worse, in such a competition in devastation, even if it could throw more bombs.

" America's allies in Europe certainly wouldn't welcome it. They may want her to defend them against invasion, but they don't relish the idea of eventual liberation by a campaign of atomic devastation—and in such a case we should take good care that they shared the affliction with us.

" To rub in the folly of a prolonged bombing match with atomic weapons—besides causing panic and confusion—it might be worth while for us at an early stage to make some

12

raids on New York and other big American cities. They are well within the radius of our new TuG-75 bomber. Our older but plentiful TU-4s modelled on the American ' Flying Fortresses ', could also reach transatlantic targets. They don't have to come back—and that enables them to make a wider detour in the approach. Our airmen are accustomed to regard ' suicide ' missions as natural in the course of duty. Moreover, they can land in Central America, whereas American airmen won't have much chance of finding refuge in Europe once we've overrun it.

" However, until our stock of atomic bombs has increased a lot, I am against using more than a few in transatlantic terror-raids. In the first stage of a war, most of them should be reserved for England, or other European countries that show stubbornness.

" England, and America's other satellite countries, all offer such crowded targets that they could be easily crippled. Thanks to Russia's immensely wider spread, and Stalin's foresight in dispersing our industrial plants, as well as our people's simpler and less luxurious way of life, we could probably survive five or ten times as many atomic bombs as our enemies could.

" But I should naturally prefer to avoid the risk and the damage, relatively less though it may be. So I would rather hold back our atomic bombing if and while our enemies hesitate to unleash theirs. We possess such great advantages in other respects. Our land forces, and supporting air forces, are amply sufficient for us to strike in all theatres simultaneously. We've got a big balance of strength *everywhere* over our opponents, and it's desirable to find useful employment for our many unmechanised divisions.

" In the Far East, I should use part of our Fourth Army, which is positioned near the Behring Strait, for a raiding stroke against Alaska. That is not a suitable line for a major operation, but even a small stroke there would play on the fears of the Americans and Canadians, and ensure a disproportionate diversion of their forces to guard their own continent.

" My main thrust would be from Sakhalin and the Kuriles, reinforced from the near-by bases on the mainland, into Japan. There's only a small strip of water on that side, and our air force should be able to dominate it. Moreover, we have eight airborne divisions available. When the American divisions from Japan were rushed into Korea in 1950, I should have liked to throw my airborne forces into Japan— thus capturing the Americans' base and isolating them. That was the perfect retort to their impetuous move in bolstering up the South Koreans—and how amusing it would have been to put MacArthur himself in the bag! But Stalin thought it would be more profitable in the long run to encourage the Americans to bring over an increasing number of troops and become so fully bogged down in Korea as to weaken their capacity to defend other and more important places.

" I can see how shrewd he was. For, as a result, our chances of overrunning Europe remain very favourable, while we should meet little serious opposition in pushing down through Iran and Irak to the Persian Gulf and the Mediterranean coast. Turkey may be a tough nut defensively, but she doesn't actually lie in the path and she hasn't got the offensive equipment to interfere effectively with our advance past her eastern flank—or, for that matter, her western flank in Europe. Overrunning the Middle East might not bring us the early use of its oil supplies, but would push our big enemies further away and provide better cover for our own oilfields in the Caucasus and new industrial plants in the Urals. At present they are uncomfortably exposed to attack from that flank.

" The only thing against our starting another Korean move

14

in the Middle East is that, now, it would probably mean war —a full-scale world war. So I have been considering where we might try a move with less certain risk of American intervention. It seems to me that the Indian area might be a favourable place. It should not be too difficult to get India and Pakistan fighting over Kashmir, and once the Pakistanis were in dire straits they might be induced to accept our 'aid'. It would be far more difficult for the Americans and British to support India in a fight started on that issue, and thus we might get well established. Our aid would, of course, go by air. The advent of the air age has much helped to transform the Indian dreams of Tsarist Russia into a realisable proposition for Soviet Russia.

" A move to Pakistan's rescue could pave the way for us to succeed the British, who succeeded the Moguls, as the rulers of India. It would also enable us to get into Southeast Asia before our present useful but potentially dangerous allies, the Chinese.

" There are such good chances of gain in various directions without a full-scale war that I would rather pursue these, in a careful way, as long as possible. That doesn't mean being timorously careful. Indeed, if I was quite sure that the Americans were going to force a show-down when their rearmament has gone further, and face us with a choice between retreat and war, I would favour striking first. For I'm not unduly worried about the outcome.

" It is astonishing how Americans assume that in such a war they are bound to win in the long run because their output of oil and steel is much greater than ours. They don't seem to realise that, with our much more limited civilian consumption, we have got an ample margin for our armaments —large as these are. Furthermore, it seems absurd to picture a *long* war carried on by atomic bombing. A mere two such bombs of elementary type crumpled up Japan, an exceptionally tough nation. I can't imagine America's complex industrial civilisation standing up to a long-duration trial of that kind.

" Thus, on balance, very favourable conclusions can be drawn from a survey of our situation in comparison with that of our opponents. Nevertheless, I would not care to advise that an invasion should be undertaken. There are too many incalculables in present weapon development. We cannot be sure enough, by Stalin's standards, of fulfilling the two basic conditions that I specified at the outset. It would therefore be wiser to pursue our camouflaged warfare policy and strategy—what our opponents call ' the cold war '—which shows many signs of continued and increasing success.

" As a Soviet soldier, I am profoundly conscious of the fundamental truth of Lenin's maxim, so masterfully applied by Stalin, that ' the soundest strategy in war is to postpone operations until the moral disintegration of the enemy renders the mortal blow both possible and easy'."

2

THE AMERICAN "NEW LOOK" IN 1954

[*This was written in April 1954, shortly after the explosion of the first H-bomb, the adoption of the doctrine of " massive retaliation " and the announcement of the American " New Look ". The warning and the criticism have been so amply confirmed by subsequent developments that its reproduction may serve to show that no exceptional foresight was required to recognise ill consequences that were so obvious at the time.*]

THE explosion of the Hydrogen Bomb this spring has cast a shadow across the free world. Those whom it is designed to protect show immensely increased anxiety. Their unhappiness is a grimly ironical reflection on the hasty and thoughtless way their leaders agreed in 1945 to unleash the atomic monster, and the even more instant decision of President Truman to go ahead with the Hydrogen Bomb.

The H-bomb might be regarded as retribution for Hiroshima—a " trigger-release " which looked to the responsible statesmen so easy and simple a way of assuring victory and subsequent world peace. The world is suffering today the consequences of their neglect to *think through* the problem.

The most urgent, and fundamental, issue on which we need to clarify our minds, *now*, is the question of what is called the " New Look " military policy and strategy. This vital question is close-coupled with the advent of the Hydrogen Bomb.

17

Just before Christmas it was announced that a new military programme, with a new strategic line, was emerging at the Pentagon and had received preliminary approval. The first accounts of it put the emphasis on the economic advantages. By 1957, manpower in the U.S. armed forces would be reduced, it was hoped, from 3,450,000 to 2,815,000—a reduction of nearly two-thirds of a million men ; roughly 18 per cent. In the Army the reduction would be 30 per cent. The saving in money would be from four to six billion dollars in the annual outlay. Economy was to be combined with efficiency. The Army would still have twenty divisions, but be streamlined, and so would the Navy. The Air Force would actually be increased in operational strength, and given priority.

The general trend of the new programme seemed good, and made sense. Anyone with knowledge, yet not mentally custom-bound, who has explored the organisation of fighting forces becomes aware of the way they always tend to accumulate superfluous fat. There was plenty of scope for slimming treatment, and also for remodelling.

But in January the new policy was given a more questionable look when the U.S. Secretary of State, Mr. Dulles, after saying that " local defence must be reinforced by the further deterrent of massive retaliatory power ", defined the new policy as a basic decision " to depend primarily on a great capacity to retaliate by means and at places of our choosing ".

Then, on the Ides of March, the New Look came to look profoundly ominous in European eyes. The Press reported Vice-President Nixon's statement that : " We have adopted a new principle. Rather than let the Communists nibble us to death all over the world in little wars, we will rely in future on massive mobile retaliatory powers."

That, all too obviously, was a threat of strategic bombing action with the new weapons of mass destruction.

The declaration sounded all the more ominous because it followed closely the explosion of the Hydrogen Bomb at Bikini on March 1. The photographs were appalling, and their effect more shattering even than the statement of the Chairman of the U.S. Atomic Energy Commission, Admiral Strauss, that *one* H-Bomb " could destroy any city ".

It may have been hoped that the explosion would impress the ruling minds in the Kremlin—but its " *back blast* " was much greater, and more measurable, for it had a shattering effect among America's European associates. The inhabitants of these " satellite " countries, so much closer to Russia and *her* strategic bombing force, were sharply reminded that seven months earlier—in August 1953—the Russians had produced an explosion of H-bomb kind. This new " Bikini suit " left them feeling completely naked.

Mr. Dulles subsequently sought to soften the impression. At a Press conference on March 16, he pointed out that in his January speech : " In no place did I say that we *would* retaliate instantly, although we might indeed retaliate instantly under conditions that call for that. The essential thing is to have the *capacity* to retaliate instantly. It is lack of that capacity which in my opinion accounted for such disasters as Pearl Harbor."

He was palpably on the proverbial horns of a dilemma between desire to reassure America's satellites and desire *not* to reassure Russia and *her* satellites—that they could, with impunity, indulge in further Korean-type aggression. But his reference to Pearl Harbor had no real relevance to such a problem of " little wars ". And any comforting effect was damped by his subsequent assertion that, the capacity for massive and instant retaliation means that " the deterrent power of that is sufficient so that you do not need to have local defence all around the 20,000-mile perimeter of the orbit of the Soviet World."

19

That argument was evidence of very confused thinking on the top levels—clearly contradictory to the experience of the years when America possessed a monopoly of atomic bombing capacity. If the argument had any substance, and is not bluff, it meant that the U.S. Government is now contemplating the employment of " massive retaliation " as an answer to Korean-type aggression.

A significant addendum to these statements was contained in the report from Washington that *The Observer* published on March 21—a date which, since 1918, has been another ominous anniversary—which stated that Mr. Dulles's conception is actually—

one which was worked out by the British Chiefs of Staff in the spring of 1952, and first presented to the American Joint Chiefs of Staff under the Chairmanship of General Bradley in June of that year by Marshal of the Royal Air Force Sir John Slessor without being accepted.

When the new Chiefs of Staff, under the chairmanship of Admiral Radford, took office last August they read the working papers and accepted the conclusions and recommendations of their British colleagues.

According to other Washington sources, the change was largely due to President Eisenhower's advent to power and Mr. Churchill's return to power. The new heads of the American and British Governments were both extremely anxious to reduce their budgets, and eagerly embraced a theory that seemed to offer the promise of saving money with security. Indeed, it is claimed that Mr. Churchill was won over to the idea even earlier, shortly before his return to power. The U.S. *Combat Forces Journal* for February had a long exposition of " The New Look Strategy ", by Mr. Lloyd Norman, which said : " After an Air Force briefing at the Pentagon on the atomic counter offensive power of the Strategic Air Command, Churchill became a total convert to atomic airpower "—citing an account in the *Quarterly Review* published by the Air War College.

When the Korean War came to a stop, the urge to econo-mise money was reinforced by the public call to " bring the boys home ". This combination of pressures, together with a natural desire to gain credit for the new Administration, im-pelled the production of a military policy that would look new.

In reality, it was little more than a reversion to the earlier policy of relying on the atomic bomb as a deterrent to aggres-sion—a policy which had been proved inadequate by the Korean test of 1950, and then been superseded by a more tangible form of protection. But the heavy expense of pro-viding such a protecting presence on the scene revived the idea of finding an improved " containment " at cheaper cost.

Its pattern was a compromise between the claims, and demands, of the three Services—Navy, Army, and Air—giving preference to the newest one without giving offence to the older Services.

It was also an attempt to reconcile three different ideas—

The concept of a quick knock-out punch by air delivery of atomic bombs in the heart of Russia.

The concept of countering invasion by Russia's vastly larger land forces through the use, on the battle-front, of the new tactical atomic bombs and shells.

The concept of containment without conflict—by deploying sufficient strength on the ground to provide an effective deterrent to aggression.

But this was an attempt to reconcile three incompatible ideas—and fuse them in a trinity that had no basic unity. Intoxication with atomic power made it look more hopeful. The comforting illusion was shattered by the explosion of the H-bomb on March 1—an appropriate date for this try-out would have been April 1 !

The H-bomb makes nonsense of the aim of pursuing " victory " in a " total war ". Both terms, and the concepts they express, now become totally absurd. Anyone who dreams

21

or talks of " winning the war ", if war should come, is worse than absurd—a menace to his country and to all humanity.

Warfare as conceived and conducted from the time of Napoleon and Clausewitz to that of Hitler and Churchill has become obsolete.

Churchill comes in that historical bracket not only because he was foremost in opposing Hitler's dream of conquest, but also because he, more than anyone else, embodied and expressed the belief that our problems could be, simply, solved by victory. After America came into the war, he spoke of himself as Roosevelt's lieutenant, and became that increasingly, but originally took the initiative in setting the aim.

His final volume on the war is entitled *Triumph and Tragedy*. The title is even more fitting than he seems aware, in his puzzled concern with secondary clues. The pursuit of triumph in such a war was foredoomed to end in tragedy, and futility—since the complete conquest of Germany at which he blindly aimed was bound to clear the way for Russia's domination of Europe, and a vast extension of Communist power in all directions.

Under *present* conditions the all-out pursuit of victory would be far worse than futile. Marshal of the R.A.F. Sir John Slessor has himself recently declared, in his broadcasts on the revolution in strategy resulting from the combination of air and atomic power: " I believe the first and most far-reaching consequence of this revolution is that total war as we have known it in the past forty years is a thing of the past . . . a world war in this day and age would be general suicide and the end of civilisation as we know it." In contrast to many who are still living in the past, he has thought his way half through the present problem—but *only* half way. For, strangely, he still regards the air-atomic combination as our trump-card against aggression.

This idea would seem to rest on an illusion. Would any

responsible government, when it came to the point, dare to *use* the H-bomb as an answer to local and limited aggression ? It would be a lunatic action to take the lead in unleashing this menace, with the likelihood of bringing on world war with H-bombs—which the air chiefs themselves realise " would be general suicide and the end of civilisation ".

Thus any threat to use it is perilous folly or empty bluff— with doubled disadvantages and boomerang effect. Mr. Walter Lippmann points out that: "It has become impossible for small or middle-sized countries within easy reach of an aggressor who is armed with atomic weapons to commit themselves to intervene in a world war." Any further threats or proposals along the " Nixon line " would be the surest way to break up the Atlantic Alliance and open the gates to Communism.

The H-bomb is more handicap than help to the policy of containment. Hence the New Look strategy really became out of date as soon as it appeared—like its namesake in the world of fashion. In each case it was an old look rehashed, expressing an over-optimistic desire for stability and tranquillity— at a time when conditions were highly unfavourable to the fulfilment of that desire.

To the extent that the H-bomb reduces the likelihood of full-scale war, it *increases* the possibilities of limited war pursued by widespread local aggression. The enemy can exploit a choice of techniques, differing in pattern but all designed to make headway while causing hesitancy about employing counteraction by H-bombs, or A-bombs.

The aggression might be at limited tempo—a gradual process of encroachment. It might be of limited depth but fast tempo—small bites quickly made, and as quickly followed by offers to negotiate. It might be of limited density—a multiple infiltration by particles so small that they formed an intangible vapour.

23

A further drawback of the H-bomb is that it may, in effect, nullify the possibility of using the tactical atomic bombs and shells on which the NATO forces have recently come to rely as an offset to Russia's much larger Army. It becomes more doubtful whether such smaller atomic weapons can be defensively used to stop advancing troops without precipitating an illimitable and suicidal H-bomb devastation of countries and cities.

It also becomes very questionable whether we can continue to contemplate *any air force action*, with ordinary high explosive bombs, *at any considerable distance* behind an aggressor's front. For if any large aircraft were reported to be flying towards the interior it might all too easily be taken as a signal that the H-bomb was on the way—and thus precipitate the immediate despatch of H-bombers from that side. The policy of " capacity to retaliate instantly ", as defined by Mr. Dulles, becomes a dangerously two-edged weapon.

These reflections, and rejections, point to the conclusion that the value of strategic bombing forces has largely disappeared—except as a last resort, if Russia should initiate such action. It is contrary to the balance of probability that she would do so, since we have more to lose than she has to gain by competitive H-bombing. For us to start it would be lunacy, yet in " coming to our senses " we are left to face the very uncomfortable fact that the abstention which sanity demands entails the forfeit, or at least the very limited use, of our strongest card.

In sum, the development of the H-bomb has weakened our power of resistance to Communist aggression. That is a very serious consequence.

For the containment of the menace we now become more dependent on conventional weapons. That conclusion, however, does not mean that we must fall back on conventional methods. It should be an incentive to the development of newer ones.

We have moved into a new era of strategy that is very different to what was assumed by the advocates of air-atomic power—the revolutionaries of the past era. The strategy now being developed by our opponents is inspired by the dual idea of evading and hamstringing superior air-power. Ironically, the further we have developed the " massive " effect of the bombing weapon, the more we have helped the progress of this new guerrilla-type strategy.

Our own strategy should be based on a clear grasp of this concept, and our military policy needs re-orientation. There is scope, and we might effectively develop it, for a counter-strategy of corresponding kind. Here one may remark in parenthesis, that to wipe out cities with H-bombs would be to destroy our potential " Fifth Column " assets.

So long as Russia has the H-bomb, coupled with a strategic air force, we are bound to cling on to this "suicidal" weapon—too dangerous to "drop" in either sense. But the general pattern of the forces we require is almost the opposite of the " New Look " trend.

Capacity to deliver the H-bomb does not depend on having a vast Strategic Air Force, as the bombing campaign of World War II required. Quality matters more than quantity and a relatively small number of super-performance aircraft would provide, inherently, a stronger guarantee of reaching the target—if that became necessary.

A realisation that the customary employment of a Strategic Bombing Force is now out of the question, or out of date, is our most urgent requirement. For it would open a way—the only possible way—to increased provision of the kind of force we do require—land, sea, and tactical air—without an increase of expenditure that is beyond our economic capacity.

The problem of security can be solved without bankruptcy—by some fresh expenditure of thought. Besides a re-distribution between the forces, there is much scope for tactical improvement and technical development in the " loco-mobility " of our ground forces in foiling our opponent's guerrilla-type strategy.

But the *basic* needs for our security are cool-headedness, patience, and capacity for thinking-through problems. Our primary risks are indignation, exasperation, and hasty thinking—a triple combination that is all too liable to detonate a fatal explosion.

3

THE BRITISH "OLD LOOK" OF 1956

THE persistence of old habits of thought, regardless of a changed situation and changing conditions, was never more clearly demonstrated than in the British response to Nasser's seizure of the Suez Canal in 1956. The countermove that was launched four months later bore an " old look " in every aspect.

Besides the declared purpose of stopping the spread of war in the Middle East, the venture had four main aims. To keep open the Suez Canal, to ensure the flow of oil supplies, to shatter Nasser's position, and to block Russian penetration.

But the outcome of the Anglo-French action was the exact reverse of its objects. The Suez Canal was blocked, the oil supplies interrupted, Nasser's position strengthened, and the way opened for further Russian penetration. The course and results of the action can be summed up, in brief, as " making the *worst* of a bad job ". In the political, the economic, and the military sense it was a compound sum of errors, each multiplying the others.

Ironically, the British Government's best answer to the charge of collusion with Israel is that this intervention deprived not only Israel but Britain of the benefits that could have come to both if it had abstained. The Israelis' retaliatory stroke against the Egyptians had gained such success and gone so far by the time the British butted in that within a few more days the Suez Canal would probably have been freed, the Egyptian airfields so destroyed that they could not

27

have been used for bringing in Russian aircraft of volunteers, and Nasser's prestige utterly demolished.

All that would have been done without any moral or material cost to Britain. She would have been on good ground in restraining Russian intervention and in helping to bring about a peaceable settlement.

It is difficult to understand how Sir Anthony Eden could have imagined that the form of his ultimatum and his follow-up action could possibly look, to anyone outside Britain, anything except a one-sided move against Egypt, to regain control of the Suez Canal.

Having taken the fateful decision, all hope of a successful result depended on *quick* success. The first essential was to secure the whole stretch of the Canal before the Egyptians had time to block it. The second was to achieve complete success before world opinion hardened against Britain and France, or Russia had a chance to intervene.

But the method of action, the tempo of action, the type of forces, and even the bases were unsuited to the purpose. That should have been obvious beforehand to the Governmen and its Service advisers.

The method was too like a miniature repetition of the Mediterranean landings in the last war, when time mattered less than careful and massive preparation. In the Suez operation, the British habit and motto "slow but sure" was all too sure to prove unsure—by being too slow.

The surest way to save the Canal from being blocked was to capture the keypoints along it, and the airfields, by a surprise drop from the sky. That required at least one airborne division, and preferably two. For years it had been urged that Britain's strategic reserve at home should be an airborne force, and that a fleet of air transport must be built up sufficient to carry a whole division—to any danger spot overseas. But despite all the urging she had only one brigade of this type, and was very short of air transport

Moreover, when it came to the point of delivering the airborne attack, at Port Said solely, only one British battalion (some 500 men) was dropped from the air, the other two being sent in by sea. The French dropped more than twice as many, and were about to drop a further 1,500 when the " cease-fire " cut short the operation. It was the more unfortunate since the British task was to open the way south along the first stretch of the Canal, while the French were to follow on and pass through at a midway point, to make the exploiting drive to the far end at Suez.

As there were not enough airborne troops to carry out the whole operation, this deficiency meant that the main force had to be brought by sea—a slower process, with consequently diminished chances of surprise.

The handicap was increased by the unsuitability of Britain's bases. Cyprus is only some 200 miles from Port Said, a day's run by sea, but has only one small harbour. Malta is nearly 1,000 miles distant, too far for a quick move, while too small for mounting a large expedition and giving the troops proper training while waiting in readiness. The ports in Libya seemed to offer a midway starting site, and figured largely in the initial plans, but when the plans became clear to the Arab inhabitants the planners were brought to realise, belatedly, that the bases there could not be used for mounting an attack on another Arab country. That applied also to Britain's bases in Jordan. So she had to fall back on the use of Malta.

In addition, the shipping difficulties were increased because her tank-landing ships were too few, and her tanks too big. Although over thirty tank-landing ships had been retained on the Navy's strength, only two were kept in operational state. Two sufficed to carry merely half a regiment of Centurion tanks, a force inadequate for any likely operation.

Many troubles, and delays occurred, with spreading consequences, in the process of " de-mothballing " landing ships laid up in reserve, and in making up the quantity required by reconverting to military use others sold to civilian firms.

The shrinking chances of surprise and speed in the operation vanished with the decision to conduct a lengthy course of bombing action before the troop landings. Not until the sixth day did these begin, with the paratroops' drop, and the landings from the sea were a day later still. Long before then the Canal was blocked, and the Anglo-French action condemned by an overwhelmingly adverse vote of the United Nations, with the United States Government taking the lead against its continuance.

How did such a fatally slow course of action come to be planned and pursued ? Primarily it was due to last war habits combined with fear of possibly heavy casualties—and of public outcry if such occurred—from counteraction by Nasser's air force, especially the interception of the transport aircraft by his jet fighters.

It is clear now that this was a much overrated risk—as a number of experts thought beforehand. But it was a basic mistake to attempt any stroke unless prepared to run such a risk, for in the case of Suez it was a lesser risk than that of forfeiting surprise and time, with consequent failure to fulfil the purpose.

Another influential factor in the prolonged bombing seems to have been an Air Staff desire to try out its favourite theory and see if the issue could be decided by air action alone. That inclination fitted in with, and fostered, the arguments of the more cautious among the Army planners.

These were not the only factors that weighed against the surprise and speed that are the essence of any such coup. National Service was a handicap, especially the need of calling up so many men from the Reserve. The muddles in mobilisation were appalling—muddles in calling up reservists, in collecting the equipment and stores supposed to be readily available on mobilisation, in providing for the waterproofing of vehicles, and in loading the ships. Much of the equipment was found to be unserviceable. Moreover ships were sent off loaded in a way unsuited to a landing on a hostile shore, as in the ill-fated Gallipoli expedition of 1915.

National character was also a handicap, for swift success in offensive action requires qualities—audacity, dynamism, and ruthlessness—that are no longer natural to the British as they were in the times of Drake and Nelson, and as they evidently are to the modern Israelis. The code name given to the operation, " Musketeer ", was all too typical of its out-of-date conception.

The military faults were bad enough. But the political and economic faults were worse.

Politically, ultimate success was impossible unless United States support was assured, in view of the adverse weight of the Afro-Asian bloc in the U.N., and the risk of Russian interference. It was rash to attempt military action against Egypt without President Eisenhower's acquiescence. So it was foolish to keep him in the dark and leave him feeling he had been tricked. His indignant reaction was very natural—what any businessman would feel if his junior partners gambled with the firm's assets behind his back.

Economically the British Government put its head in a double noose. For it could not carry on, nor even survive, without American aid to meet its oil and financial needs. It was foolish to start a war that it could not afford, even if it succeeded, without any assurance of that essential aid.

As it was, it could not even have afforded to continue it for another week without financial disaster—the collapse of sterling. That hard fact is the decisive answer to the argument, which still continues, that it should have pushed on with its venture regardless of the United Nations and the United States.

What is the final lesson of Suez ? That Britain is no longer fitted to play the amoral game of " power-politics ". The checks inherent in her democratic system, moral scruples, and difficulty in carrying ruthlessness to an extreme, form a triple handicap. This is multiplied by slow-motion habits. On top of all is her present economic dependence on the U.S. So it is better in every sense for her to follow a moral policy—or at least a policy likely to be supported by the majority of world opinion.

BRITAIN'S " BIG BLUFF "

" Land of Hope and Glory " was long a favourite British lyric, with its refrain :

> Wider still and wider shall thy bounds be spread,
> God who made thee mighty, make thee mightier yet.

Earlier generations gazing at the map of Britain's world-wide possessions used to talk of " the empire on which the sun never sets ". That was their favourite boast. They were unconscious that exactly the same phrase had once been used about the now long vanished empires of Spain and Portugal, and earlier still about the Roman Empire.

The most extraordinary thing about the British Empire was that such a small island with such a small Army, and spending so little on its forces, succeeded for so long in ruling such vast and densely populated regions, in distant parts of the world. It was an astonishing achievement—and the biggest bluff in all history.

It was a bluff from the start, but at least it had a basis of real strength, even though this was far from being proportionate to the tremendous results it produced. The sea power, machine power, and money power that Britain developed, especially after the Industrial Revolution, laid the foundation of her imperial expansion. Accumulated prestige put a roof on the structure, and also an impressive face.

Her land forces were kept small to save money, but their weapons were good enough to give them a dominating advantage over primitively armed masses in Asia and Africa. That was not astonishing, for in the sixteenth century, when firearms were a novelty, a mere 600 Spanish soldiers conquered the Aztec Empire in Mexico while less than 200 sufficed to overthrow the Peruvian Empire.

Britain's naval forces were usually strong enough to ensure command of the sea, and thus to keep other European Powers from intervening.

Her growing financial resources were a strong asset, and often a valuable aid in winning native supporters.

The British were aided also in many cases by the readiness of the population to greet them as a relief from their native tyrants, and they then made their own rule more acceptable by just administration of the countries.

But when this present century came the *material* basis of of the " big bluff " was weakened by the intrusion of new factors. Britain's control of the sea was threatened by the rise of new naval Powers. Among these was Japan, an Asiatic country, whose navy she had built and trained as an offset to her European rivals, but whose victories against Russia in 1904–5 made the first big crack in " white " prestige. Then seapower itself was shaken by the advent of airpower.

Meanwhile the *psychological* basis of the bluff was undermined by the spread of Western-like education, and by bringing many of the younger men to be educated in England. On returning home they often felt frustrated by lack of full opportunity, especially political, and galled by a sense of being regarded as inferior. British officials' air of superiority could all too easily outweigh the solid benefits of British rule. At the same time the British were becoming less ruthless than of old in suppressing revolt, and even when the will to do so continued the spread of news by Press and radio made ruthlessness more difficult as a policy.

The *military* hollowness of the empire's defence became obvious in the nineteen-thirties—except to the people of Britain and its Government. Yet on a close examination it was disturbingly clear that her forces, even if they could be doubled, would still be inadequate to cover such a widespread empire against the many new threats that had developed.

The bluff was shattered when the Second World War came—by the disasters suffered in the Far East at the hands of the Japanese, and to a lesser extent by the defeats that Rommel inflicted in the Middle East about the same time.

It was both tragedy and irony that the chance of preserving Malaya and Burma was forfeited by Churchill's fateful decision that reinforcements should be sent to the Middle East in 1941—to seek a victory there that was not achieved —at the expense of what was needed to save Singapore and the position in the Far East.

The effect of these disasters and defeats were not retrieved, nor Britain's prestige, by ultimate victory in 1945. For in the world's eyes, if not in hers, that victory was won mainly by the converging weight of America and Russia. Moreover, victory left them confronting each other as the two great world powers, while it left Britain exhausted by the prolonged overstrain of her smaller resources. It also left Britain a bankrupt dependent on America's charity. Yet in the post-war years she still struggled to play the role of a great power in the military realm. The vain attempt proved a diminished resurrection of the old bluff, fooling only herself, while hampering her economic recovery.

The case for a new line of policy is reinforced by military realism. Britain cannot *defend* the Middle East. Not even with American aid. Russia's forces available for use there are vastly larger than those which could oppose her. Russia could easily spare twenty or more divisions for a double-prong invasion, from the Caucasus and east of the Caspian. Her airborne divisions, of which she is reported to have ten, with 7,500 transport planes—form the ideal " tin-opener " for quickly forcing mountain barriers, seizing keypoints deep in rear, and spreading panic.

For meeting such a blow, the armies of the Arab States are little more than a paper-screen. While Turkey is more capable of self-defence, she lies " off the edge ", and could not bar the path to the Middle East oilfields.

What could the West do to reinforce the defence? Britain and France could perhaps send two divisions and the United States a further two, but even this small number could not be sent wholly and immediately by air. So it would be another case of " too little and too late ". The Allies may hope to stop an invasion by nuclear bombing and shelling of the mountain passes, but that might prove only a partial check. Russia's airborne forces are the means to jump over such a block, while ample to smash any opponents—and capture the oilfields.

In sum, the only military way of keeping the Russian Army out of the Middle East is by *deterrence*—deterring invasion by fear of H-bombs dropping on Russia's own vital centres.

Moreover, Britain is now left without suitable bases—and to build fresh bases, if she could find them, would carry no better prospect. The attempt would only inflame anti-British feelings and suspicions, especially after Suez, and thus aid the Russians' political infiltration—the underlying danger.

The best hope of countering Russian influence, and of preserving Britain's oil supplies from the Middle East, may be for her to take up the detached role of " the good customer ".

The Far East, too, is undefendable in the real sense. Moreover China, being more primitively organised, is less vulnerable than Russia to the nuclear deterrent. Yet Britain continues to cling on to Imperial footholds in that area which are crumbling underneath her, sapped by the tide of Asiatic nationalism.

By " cutting out " militarily, she would save an immense amount of vain expense, and at the same time reduce her risks. With a small fraction of the saving she could pay such a good price for raw materials as to become " the customer whom it pays to please ". By contrast, the longer she tarries the heavier her sacrifice is likely to be—without compensation.

Experience should have taught Britain by now the folly of standing on crumbling sand castles all over the world. If she profits by the lesson, and learns to keep within the limits of her strength, that strength is likely to increase again—with good prospects. This is also the way to regain the influence she has lost by living in dreams of past glory and pretending to power that she no longer possesses.

PART TWO
PROSPECT

4

THE SPUTNIK AND THE LUNIK

SINCE the Russian sputniks and their carrier rockets began circling the world, their radio signals have been telling the peoples of the world that no defence exists. Their gentle " bleep bleep " has been the loudest and most shattering blast since the trumpets of Joshua and the shout of his people flattened the walls of Jericho. The " bleep " has cracked the foundations of Western defence planning.

When the Russians announced in August 1957 that they had successfully launched an ICBM (inter-continental ballistic missile), and could " direct rockets into any part of the world ", their claim was doubted in various quarters—particularly in America. When the satellite was successfully launched early in October, the first reaction in such quarters was to discount its significance. The professional head of the U.S. Navy scornfully referred to it as " only a hunk of iron which anyone could launch ". Even after the second and bigger satellite had been launched, Field-Marshal Montgomery was reported in an interview as saying : " Don't be afraid of the sputnik. I say the satellites do not give Russia any strategic or military predominance."

That was true in the direct and narrow sense, but indirectly and psychologically this demonstration of Russia's lead in the rocket field was of immense strategic and politico-military importance.

For it had long been taken as a certainty by the NATO countries in Europe that the United States possessed a big

39

superiority over Russia in A-bombs, H-bombs, and their means of delivery—even if the margin of advantage might be shrinking. It was therefore assumed that this American nuclear superiority amply counterbalanced the Russians' much larger army, and would suffice to deter them from attempting to invade any country that America had taken under its protective wing. A third assumption was that, at the worst, the United States strategic air force could defeat any attack.

A doubt about these comforting assumptions had been growing for some time past. The sputnik made them look like delusions. Launching a satellite successfully into a global orbit required, and showed, a great accuracy in the aiming and guiding of the carrier rocket, as well as a great development in size and proportion of rockets. It went far to confirm the earlier Russian statements about their new inter-continental rocket. To the public everywhere it served as convincing proof of the Russians' ability to hit large targets, such as cities form, in any of the Western countries.

Then at the start of 1959 came the successful launching of the Russian moon-rocket on January 2. A great scientific achievement, and in itself of a peaceful kind, the *lunik* was a triumph for Russian science even greater than the first *sputnik* launched fifteen months earlier. Its performance was the more shining by contrast with the initial failures, in turn, of the American earth-satellites and moon-rockets.

There has now been ample time to assess the scientific evidence provided by the Russians' achievement, and from that to deduce its wider bearing on the strategic situation of the Western Powers in relation to Soviet Russia. The military, psychological, and political effects on their defence are potentially tremendous. They have been given too little attention in the governing circles of the West. This inadequate response in the reconsideration of their strategic policy would be astonishing if it were not all too characteristic of the way that the leaders of the Western countries, then headed by France and Britain, ignored the revolutionary implications of mechanised warfare a generation earlier, and the warning then blazoned for anyone whose eyes were open.

The reaction of the Western countries to the latest warning message, given by the sputnik and the moon-rocket, has been like that of valley-dwellers awakened by the bursting of a dam, and then falling asleep again without thought that a flood is pouring down on their house.

Time after time the Russians have proved successful in reaching some fresh stage of scientific or technical development years before they were expected to achieve it.

When the Americans took the fateful decision to use the first atomic bomb at Hiroshima, to hasten Japan's surrender, they took little account of the risk that it might become a boomerang, through stimulating others to match such a weapon of wholesale destruction. When tension with Russia became acute, in the Berlin crisis of 1948, the Americans still showed a happy confidence that their monopoly of the atomic bomb would continue for years ahead, even as long as ten years. They scoffed at Russian statements early in 1949 which conveyed a broad hint that Russia had succeeded in developing a similar weapon. Yet in August that year their own instruments detected an atomic explosion in Russia which showed that their monopoly had been broken. Moreover, that was three years ahead of the first British atomic bomb becoming ready for test.

The worst shock came in August 1953—August seems to be an ominous month—when the Russians exploded a fusion device of what is called the H-bomb kind. That was only nine months after the first American test explosion of such a kind (and four years before the first British test explosion). It showed how fast the Russians were going ahead, for their comparative time-lag in developing an atomic bomb had been four years.

Official complacency about America's lead in atomic weapon-power still reappears at intervals, although now based on the assumption that she must still be well ahead of the Russians in quantity, if not in quality. That comforting assumption is habitually expressed at NATO conferences. It ignores the hard fact that a Western superiority in the number of bombs would be of no avail if the Russians have, and can deliver, the relatively small number that would be sufficient to wreck and devastate the Western countries, which are more densely populated and vulnerable than Russia. Superiority in these fatal weapons means little in face of such sufficiency.

But now a new and much bigger question has arisen—whether the NATO countries can rely any longer on the protection hitherto provided by the deterrent power of the U.S. strategic air force. For the performance of the moon-rocket, following on that of the sputniks, demonstrated that the Russians had developed a system of guiding large rockets, at immensely long ranges, far more accurate than the Americans had yet evolved. The Russians are the masters in the rocket field, and have established a lead that will be hard to overtake.

An error of only 2 per cent. in aiming at a target nearly a quarter of a million miles away, and subject to time complications as well as gravitational pulls, was an astonishing degree of precision—ten times better than the Americans expected in their attempted moon shot a few months earlier. A power that possesses such an accurate system should have little difficulty in delivering hydrogen bombs, at a range of 3,000–5,000 miles, close enough to the great cities and industrial areas of America to wreck them, and wipe out most of their population.

The moon-rocket was shattering to faith in the superiority of American weapon-power, and in the protection thus promised against aggression. It was the bursting of the dam that covered the NATO valley. The effect could be catastrophic psychologically, even if not physically, if the slumbering inhabitants awake to reality suddenly in a crisis.

This does not mean that the West's nuclear power, embodied mainly in the U.S. Strategic Air Command, has completely ceased to be a deterrent, and protection. It remains a deterrent to, and thereby an indirect protection against, *nuclear* attack so long as the capacity for retaliation is sufficient to ensure that any surprise blow—any attempt at a nuclear Pearl Harbor stroke—is likely to prove mutually suicidal.

But it has become doubtful whether this former " Great Deterrent " remains a sufficient deterrent to lesser forms of aggression, or even to a strong invasion with conventional forces.

For nuclear parity leads to nuclear nullity—because the suicidal boomerang result of using such weapons induces strategic sterility. Moreover, parity in this sphere does not require equality in numbers—of bombs and their carriers— but only the capability of delivering the minimum, a very low minimum, that would suffice to wreck the mainspring of the main power on the other side—the capital and great industrial centres. The mere probability is paralysing and sterilising. Indeed, it is ironically apt that an alternative meaning of the word " parity " is " the condition or fact of having borne offspring ". By giving birth to the atomic bomb, America gained a temporary strategic advantage, but the sequel has been to annul her potency.

Nuclear nullity inherently favours and fosters a renewal of non-nuclear aggressive activity—a field in which America and her European allies are much weaker than their opponents as a result of having pinned so much faith for so long to supremacy in nuclear power.

Now that New York and Chicago are within range of bombardment by Russian rockets, with nuclear warheads, would not the Americans hesitate to unleash their strategic air force in reply to Russian aggression in Europe or Asia ? Such hesitation would be very natural, unless the attack was obviously on a great scale and far-reaching in aim. When it came to the point, would any nation invite its own destruction if the danger did not look vital ?

What would have been regarded as vital in the old days may not be considered really vital in face of the prospect of nuclear warfare—with its fatal consequences for all concerned. Many times in the past, nations have believed, and governments have defined, some oversea position in their sphere of interest as a vital interest, and made heavy sacrifices to preserve it—and then, after losing it, have found that the loss was not fatal to them, as they had feared. Indeed, they have often been able to carry on quite well without it.

For generations, British statesmen of all parties habitually described the Mediterranean route to the East via the Suez Canal as vital to Britain, and as her " life line ". Yet in World War II they were forced—and proved able—to abandon it for three years as a sea route, diverting all regular traffic round the Cape of Good Hope. After the war, they again began to call it vital—and Mr. Bevin, when Foreign Minister, declared that to lose control of the Suez Canal would be " cutting our throat ". Yet in 1956 it was snatched away from Britain—and, after an abortive effort to regain control, she gave up the attempt in face of the greater risk of bringing on a nuclear war. France had taken a similar view about the vital importance of Indo-China. Both losses were damaging, but not deadly.

With the development of such catastrophic weapons as H-bombs, even the strongest nations are likely to become more cautious in their views of what is vital—especially if it comes to a question of putting their views into execution. In conference it is easy to draw lines on the map, and declare that any infringement of them will immediately result in massive retaliation with nuclear weapons. But it would be unrealistic for the smaller countries to take it for granted that their big protector will take such extreme action instantly and without hesitation, on their behalf, now that his own land is within reach of a reply bombardment. Any responsible government would be inclined to hesitate.

Unfortunately, Russia's rulers are shrewd enough to realise the likelihood of such hesitation. Worse still, they may become increasingly inclined to count on it. On that reckoning they may further develop, and exploit, politico-military techniques of making headway while causing hesitation—nibbling into the Western positions without looking as though they intended to swallow them entire.

Here lies the inherent weakness of the theory of massive retaliation by air coupled with " trip-wire " ground forces, just sufficient to act as a warning signal and momentary check in case of any sudden attack or encroachment. This was the theory which the Western Powers embraced in 1954. It appeared to offer a way of combining effectiveness with economy—and so was the more eagerly accepted, with too little reflection. Now it looks as if the more likely effect will be to trip up ourselves.

There is urgent need of a better kind of deterrent that does not impale us on the horns of the dilemma: " Suicide or Surrender." It must be a more workable kind of deterrent—one that could be put into operation as a defence, against anything less than an all-out attack. The better it is potentially as a *defence*, in a non-suicidal way, the surer it promises to be as a *deterrent*.

45

A main hindrance to its development has been the persistence of military concepts that are really no more than old
habits of thought. They have, in turn, produced an inflated
idea of the financial burden involved in combining a non-
nuclear defence, and immediate deterrent, with the ultimate
nuclear deterrent. For so long as soldiers still think in terms
of a lengthy war, and of winning it, they tend to put the
requirements—in men, equipment, and money—much higher
than the statesmen feel that they can meet.

5

BASIC PROBLEMS OF WESTERN DEFENCE

A FUNDAMENTAL question underlies any, and all, plans of Western defence. Can Europe, or even America, be *defended*? The answer—if we are honest, and brave enough to face hard facts—can only be that, in the present conditions, effective defence is not possible.

For defence in the real sense of the word, as defined in dictionaries, means to " preserve, protect, keep safe, by resisting attack ". At present if nuclear weapons of megaton power are actually used, no country can hope to keep safe, or even to avoid fatal destruction.

The essential conclusion was put very clearly by the British Prime Minister in 1957, at a dinner given in London to welcome General Norstad as the new Supreme Allied Commander, Europe. For Mr. Macmillan there said—

Let us be under no illusion; military forces today are not designed to wage war; their purpose is to prevent it. There will be no campaigns again like the old ones, with victory at the end of a long and balanced struggle ; total war today can only mean total destruction.

This basic fact should be kept constantly in mind when examining each aspect of the problem.

THE PROBABLE CONDITIONS OF NUCLEAR WAR

Experience of the last war can be more of a handicap than a help in visualising what might happen in a war waged with nuclear weapons. Experience in conducting operations or in military administration during that war can be even more a handicap, because of the habits of thought and practice developed in those conditions. Even the worst bombing, and resulting dislocation, were not comparable to the probable effects of nuclear warfare. Reason and imagination can hardly bridge the gulf.

The largest bombs used in Europe during the last war were no more than five to ten tons, and in the largest scale attacks —with forces up of a thousand aircraft—about 5,000 tons were dropped. The first atomic bomb, dropped on Hiroshima in August 1945, had an explosive force equivalent to 20,000 tons. Thus even in the infancy of nuclear warfare a single bomber could exert four times as much destructive power as a thousand had done previously.

Only two nuclear bombs have yet been used in war. But production in quantity has been going on ever since then, and development in destructive power has been much greater still. The first operational hydrogen bomb, tested in March 1954, is known to have released an explosive force equivalent to twenty million tons—a thousand times greater than the original atomic bomb that was dropped on Hiroshima.

But by then such immense destructive power had ceased to be an American preserve. For seven months earlier, in August 1953, Soviet Russia had demonstrated that she had developed weapons of similar kind, with an explosive force measured in millions of tons (megatons) instead of thousands (kilotons).

One such bomb can destroy the largest city. Only a few would have to reach their targets in order to wipe out the main centres of industry and population in any country of western or southern Europe. Even one or two might suffice to paralyse the life of such countries, when account is taken of the vast stretch of the " fall-out " of deadly radioactive dust, as well as of the shattering moral effect.

If such weapons are actually used in war it is unimaginable that the war could continue, even in the " broken-back " way of which Sir Winston Churchill talked in 1954—a term and a concept that still persist despite their palpable unreality. For the conduct of war is a matter of *organised action*, which would be impossible in such a state of chaos. The NATO " shield forces " could not hope to maintain a defence when their sources of supply were destroyed, and their whole purpose would vanish once their homelands were destroyed. Any survivors would be fully occupied in collecting food and controlling mobs of starving refugees.

THE PROSPECTS OF DEFENCE AGAINST NUCLEAR ATTACK ?

This question can be answered very briefly—the prospects are utterly inadequate. Even in 1954 the recently created Air Defense Command of the United States openly admitted that even " a 90 per cent. effective defense might not be good enough to guarantee national survival "—and went on to say that fifty thermo-nuclear bombs " could be enough to paralyse the country, its industrial machine and its will to go on fighting ". Other authorities consider that less than a dozen might prove enough. But a 90 per cent. effective defence is only a distant hope. Dealing with the near future, the Chairman of the Joint Committee on Atomic Energy said : " At best—and this is very optimistic—we might intercept as many as one out of every four Soviet bombers."

It would be much easier for such bombers to reach and annihilate the more accessible vital centres of countries in Europe. In face of a menace of this scale, the NATO schemes of air defence and civil defence are no more than trifling with the problem.

In the case of Britain, where the vital targets are closely grouped, five to ten hydrogen bombs would almost certainly suffice to annihilate all its main centres of industry, compris-

49

ing half the population of the country. Even fewer would suffice to wipe out the vital centres of France, Belgium, Holland, and Western Germany. Moreover, such calculations are confined to material effects. It is wise to bear in mind that paralysis, and collapse can be produced by moral effect even where destruction does not take place.

To avert such a catastrophe, air defence would need to attain almost 100 per cent. effectiveness at the outset, and that is hardly conceivable. Even if a 100 per cent. effective anti-aircraft missile could be produced on the scale required to annul all attacks by bombers, there is no early hope of a counter to the ballistic rocket. The problem of countering the bomber has also become worse with the development of the " stand-off " bomb that can be launched a thousand miles away from its target.

As for Civil Defence—the reduction of a nation's *vulnerability*—the steps taken, or contemplated, by Governments during the past fifteen years have been utterly inadequate to meet attack with even a small number of atomic bombs of Hiroshima scale. The development of the hydrogen bomb has obviously made the *need* much greater. But it has also made the problem so much greater that the measures now required, besides involving expenditure vastly heavier than any national economy could bear, would demand such a tremendous alteration of the whole structure of Western civilisation as to be, in a practical sense, impossible. One cannot see our people, or any people, changing their habits and way of life to the extent required. Measures that are basically inadequate merely tend to foster fatal illusions.

THE NEW MENACE OF ROCKET BOMBARDMENT

In my 1946 book *The Revolution of Warfare* I argued that the greatest potentialities of the future lay in the rocket bomb, and that " the maintenance of a heavy-bomber force becomes a superfluity in the rocket and atomic age ". In more recent years I repeatedly emphasised that, even at a moderate rate of development, it was reasonable to expect that by 1956 the Russians would be able, at the least, to bombard London and any other of the great cities of western Europe.

But such arguments made little impression in Western quarters until that autumn—when Marshal Bulganin emphasised, in his threatening message to Sir Anthony Eden during the Suez crisis, that Britain was well within range of rocket bombardment from Russian launching sites. Then in the following February Britain's Minister of Defence, Mr. Duncan Sandys, publicly confirmed that there was " every reason to believe " that the Russians had developed a " rocket with a nuclear warhead " and that " the range of this rocket would probably be sufficient to reach Britain ".

By then, that admission understated the grim reality. For it was known from radar-traced flights that Russian rockets were reaching targets 800 to 1,000 miles distant. Moreover, the Russians had successfully tested a rocket with a range of 1,500 miles—sufficient to reach any of the American strategic bomber bases in North Africa and the Middle East.

Next, on August 26, 1957, the Russians announced : " A super long-distance, inter-continental, multi-stage ballistic rocket was launched a few days ago ". " Covering a vast distance in a brief time, the rocket landed in a target area. The results obtained showed that it is possible to direct rockets into any part of the world." Those were the key words of an announcement that startled the world. The shock was all the greater, since it came soon after the first test launching of an American inter-continental rocket, the 5,000 mile range Atlas, which ended in failure.

The immediate reaction in some high quarters was to suggest that the Russian announcement was a bluff, or at least exaggerated. But General Schriever, the American missile chief, significantly remarked : " Russia seldom lies in its announcements to the outside world. When they said they had the atom bomb, they had it. When they said they had the so-called hydrogen bomb, they had it."

The sceptics were soon confounded by the success of the Sputnik, followed by that of the Lunik. The implications have been set forth in the previous chapter.

They were significantly endorsed by Britain's new Minister of Defence, Mr. Harold Watkinson, in the opening speech of the Defence Debate of February 29, 1960—" leap day "— when he emphasised the difficulties of the defence problem, and said—

... turn to Mr. Khrushchev's recent claim to have successfully fired rockets into the Pacific with an accuracy of $1\frac{1}{2}$ miles over a range of more than 6,500 nautical miles. I am advised that such firing could be well within the technical capabilities of the Russians.

It thus becomes clearer than ever that the only protection of the Western countries lies in deterring the Russians from launching an attack—by being able to retaliate with H-bombs. But it must again be emphasised that, whatever the value of such a power as a *deterrent* to enemy attack, it is of no real value as a *defence*. For if it were *used* it would merely result in mutual suicide. That would be the inevitable outcome of war with H-bombs.

THE PROSPECTS OF DETERRENCE

A powerful bombing force, armed with nuclear bombs, is a very strong deterrent to any attempt at delivering a knock-out blow with nuclear bombs or rockets, or even at over-running the NATO countries by ground forces. For it would be the most hazardous gamble for Russia, or any other country, to base a war-plan on the belief that the other side's power of retaliation could be nullified by a surprise blow— a new Pearl Harbor coup.

A sudden and complete knock-out blow would be far more difficult to achieve than in 1941—and that had only a temporary success. For it would be almost impossible to ensure that every bomber on the opposing side is disabled, whereas even a few bombers that survived would be able, with H-bombs, to inflict tremendous destruction in reply.

To bank on nullifying the other side's power of retaliation would be as foolish as staking one's life on picking out needles in a haystack. For bombers can be distributed over many airfields. They can also, with the development of new means of vertical or short-length take-off, be launched from small airstrips scattered throughout the countryside. The dream of a complete knock-out at the start of the war has become even more absurd with the development of ballistic rockets that can be launched from anywhere on land or sea or air.

Unfortunately, this needle in a haystack problem also makes nonsense of the belief long cherished by Allied military planners—in the Pentagon, at SAC, and at SHAPE—that if the bombers of the U.S. Strategic Air Command were unleashed, they could annul Russia's power of nuclear attack within a few days. So we are brought back again to the conclusion that the only hope of preserving Europe lies in preventing war—and no longer, as in the past, in being able to win a war.

As for the prospects of success in preventing war, their best foundation is formed, ironically, by the lack of any firm foundation for aggressive planning—and the likelihood that the outcome would be as fatal to the attacker as it would be to his victim. It is the basic *uncertainty* of the outlook that does most to strengthen the existing deterrent to aggression —and particularly to any Russian attempt to overrun the free countries of Europe.

There appear to be only two conditions in which a deliberately planned onslaught would become more likely—

One is a change in American policy towards a renewed " isolationism ", leading the United States Government to withdraw its forces from Europe, and revert to a detached attitude towards what happens in Europe.

It has long been thought that the development of inter-continental missiles would foster the American people's inclination to quit Europe. But Russia's success in gaining the lead with inter-continental missiles has tended to produce the opposite effect—making the Americans more anxious to stay in Europe in order to keep Russia within reach of counter-bombardment by the shorter, medium range missiles which they have developed.

The second condition is the possible discovery and development by Soviet Russia of an effective means of countering, and *nullifying*, NATO nuclear retaliation against Russia's territory, and forces. The situation would become perilously ill-balanced if Russia produced such a means in advance of the Western Alliance.

The United States have made much progress in developing anti-aircraft guided missiles to counter bomber aircraft, and it is all too possible that Russia has made similar progress. If Russia should produce an effective antidote to the bomber, and thus nullify the West's power of massive retaliation, while at the same time possessing the power herself of bombarding the Western countries with atomic rockets, they would be reduced to a state of helplessness. Even the necessity of reckoning that this dual possibility may be a reality is sufficient to have a paralysing effect on their policy and strategy.

But to gain the *certainty* of a decisive advantage Russia would have to produce the counter not only to bombers but to ballistic rockets, and to be sure that the antidote was 100 per cent. effective—which, fortunately, is a distant and dubious possibility.

At present, the Western Powers' capacity for nuclear retaliation should suffice to deter Russia from launching a large-scale invasion of free Europe, or from attempting to paralyse the Allies' retaliatory power by a surprise blow. But, unfortunately, this power of retaliation is far less sure of proving a deterrent to smaller scale aggression. It is thus much less of an insurance against the risk of an unintentional slide into an all-out war of mutual suicide.

This risk will be increased if the Russians should become increasingly confident that they have secured a definite lead in developing long-range rockets—that might tempt them to take a bolder and more provocative line of foreign policy.

Meanwhile the risk is certainly being increased by the way that the military heads of NATO have tended to concentrate on planning and preparing for all-out nuclear war, without taking due account of more limited but more likely forms of aggression.

THE CONFUSION OF DEFENCE PLANNING

Even in planning defence in the nuclear age, the Western strategists show lack of realism. Their exercises and war-games are still governed by the old picture of a prolonged war. In all solemnity they try to work out the course of operations from H+30 (days), H+60, H+90. It is astonishing evidence of the persisting influence of habit—but it makes no sense.

Such a picture takes too little account of what would have happened in the NATO countries during a duel with nuclear weapons, however brief it may be. It is very obvious that the military planners' reason and imagination, conditioned by habits of thought developed in World War II, fail to grasp the difference between that and a war where even small nuclear weapons can produce a thousand Hiroshimas within a few hours, or where one weapon of megaton power will have a thousand times the force of the original Hiroshima bomb.

Shortly after the adoption of the policy of massive retaliation and of tactical atomic weapons, Field-Marshal Montgomery stated : " I want to make it absolutely clear that we at SHAPE are basing all our operational planning on using atomic and thermo-nuclear weapons in our defence. With us it is no longer : ' They may possibly be used.' It is very definitely : ' They will be used, if we are attacked.' " Yet a few sentences later he stated that : " There is no sound Civil Defence organisation in the national territory of any NATO nation "—and added that unless such security exists " a nation will face disaster in a world war, since the home front will collapse ".

It was extremely illogical that the heads of SHAPE should have based *all* their operational planning on a course of action that, even in their view, was bound to result in collapse. Yet the statesmen of the Western nations endorsed this planning policy.

Field-Marshal Montgomery's declaration of it was made in a lecture ominously entitled " A Look Through A Window at World War III ", and he pictured this as a prolonged struggle in three phases, ending in victory and the enemy's surrender—as in World War I and II. Repeatedly, throughout his lecture, he used the traditional terms " win the battle " and " win the war ", and talked of thus " bringing the war to a successful conclusion ". These are out-of-date terms and concepts, in the atomic age—almost as out of date as the tactics of World War I.

Present defence planning has become unrealistic, and dangerously unrealistic, particularly since the development of thermo-nuclear weapons. Yet one can sympathise with the planners in their effort to adapt military doctrine to the super-revolutionary effects of atomic energy. Some of them, however, can see things more clearly than they care to admit publicly. In a discussion of this kind on planning some years ago, one of the most acute-minded air chiefs shatteringly remarked to the generals and admirals present: " It is no use trying to plan anything beyond the first six hours of another war."

The military heads of the Western Alliance have been very slow in realising the need of giving Governments and peoples some reason to hope that the defence, if put into operation, will not automatically entail suicide. Nothing could be more damping to determination, and more conducive to hesitation, than the public statements that the heads of SHAPE have made about their plans. They have created a widespread, and still persisting, impression that they are planning to loose off nuclear weapons immediately in case of *any* attack—and not only against the attacking forces but against the countries behind.

The announcement of such plans has naturally increased the uneasiness of the peoples of free Europe, in view of the vulnerability of their own cities and more densely populated countries to nuclear devastation—which they may also suffer from nuclear weapons used in their defence.

It sounds all too like an insane reversal of the proverb " those who live in glass houses should not throw stones ". To tell the peoples that NATO can produce no better defence plan than to throw such stones is the surest way to make them hesitate about resisting aggression, to shake their determination, and to diminish their efforts to build up their forces for defence.

Confusion in the planning has been increased, and public anxiety deepened, by the introduction of what are called tactical atomic weapons. This is a general term for weapons of this tremendously destructive kind that are intended for use in the fighting zone of the armies, or against their immediate lines of supply and reinforcement.

A new, and very dangerous, complication has arisen from the decision in 1954 to equip the NATO ground forces, and their supporting " tactical " air forces, with such weapons. It increases the risk that even a local conflict might soon develop into a war of mutual annihilation—unintended by either side.

The main argument in 1950 for building up the NATO land forces and tactical air forces—at immense effort and expenditure—was that they would provide an effective and safer substitute for the atomic bomb as a deterrent to aggression. That argument is cancelled out by the adoption of atomic weapons for the use of these forces. For the military heads of NATO have made it all too clear that they do not believe that it is possible to distinguish between the tactical and strategic use of nuclear action.

The argument for providing the NATO forces with tactical atomic weapons has been that these weapons are essential to counterbalance the Soviet Army's much larger numbers of men. That was brought out in Montgomery's original announcement: " The reason for this action is that we cannot match the strength that could be brought against us unless we use nuclear weapons."

The soldiers responsible for defence planning naturally desire the maximum possible insurance, and it is not their responsibility to judge whether the *apparent* increase of battlefield insurance offered by atomic weapons is outweighed by the increased risk of chaos and collapse in the homelands.

In bowing to the military argument for such extra insurance the statesmen may hopefully think that they can restrain its employment until the need is certain. But this is a frail hope. There is much greater risk in equipping armies with atomic weapons than air forces, since armies are posted in more advanced positions.

Commanders will always tend to use every weapon they possess rather than risk their troops being overrun—and in that immediate concern are apt to lose sight of wider issues. Moreover, once doctrine and organisation are established on a particular weapon-basis an almost irresistible pressure is generated. Such pressure becomes all the more certain now that field artillery weapons can be provided with atomic ammunition

But the possible benefits are outweighed by the drawbacks and dangers, unless we can find a way of establishing a dividing line between tactical and strategical action with such weapons—so that they could be used without precipitating a holocaust of the homelands with H-bombs, and civilisation's suicide.

The value of armies is essentially that of providing a non-suicidal safeguard against attack. To arm them with atomic weapons is to weaken the case for maintaining them. In that form they would increase the risks of spreading a local conflict into a general conflagration without diminishing the fatal prospect.

Even on the very dubious assumption that both sides would continue to refrain from unloosing the atomic weapon against the homelands, the NATO forces might easily lose more than they could gain from initiating the use of it in the military field. For they are largely dependent on overseas supply for their maintenance—and nothing is more vulnerable to atomic bombardment than seaport bases.

To sum up—there could be much value in the adoption of tactical nuclear weapons if, by doubling the resisting power of the present NATO armies, they made it possible to repulse an invasion by the Communists' much larger armies *without* causing the general destruction by H-bombs of the countries on either side. But there is no sense in adding such costly tactical weapons to the armoury if they are not considered a practicable *alternative* to strategic nuclear bombardment, and are likely to lead to all-out war—as the Western military leaders themselves appear to assume.

THE PROBLEM OF " GRADUATED DETERRENCE "

The insanity of planning a defence that is bound to be suicidal soon became so obvious, except to the planners themselves, that it prompted a growing number of thoughtful minds to consider the possibility of graduated action, or " graduated deterrence " as it has come to be described—unleashing H-bombs only if it is clear that the enemy is making an unlimited attack and cannot be stopped by any lesser means.

The consequences of unlimited war with nuclear weapons are so frightful that the prospect causes hesitation, delay, and feebleness in reacting to any aggression which is not obviously a vital threat. Thus the Western Allies would have a firmer balance and better prospect if they had an intermediate course—a policy of graduated deterrence and a plan of graduated action, based on the principle of applying the *minimum* force *necessary* to repel any particular aggression and deter an extension of this. Such a graduated policy would not exclude nuclear retaliation as an ultimate resort, but its action would be directed primarily against the forces engaged in the aggression—using tactical means only, and thus avoiding the strategic bombing of cities.

The prevalent idea that any such limitation of nuclear action requires, and depends on, an " agreement " with the enemy is mistaken. Nor does it call for our commitment to a binding pledge. It only requires that our policy and practice should be sufficiently clear that mutual limitation is likely, as the only way to avoid common annihilation. The development of the hydrogen bomb, and growing awareness of the mutually fatal effect of releasing it, is the best guarantee of mutual restraint.

What are the possible drawbacks of such an alternative policy? It has been argued that if a potential aggressor could feel sure that the Western powers would not launch H-bomb retaliation in immediate retort to aggression, such assurance would diminish the present deterrent, and increase the likelihood of war. By now, however, the Communist leaders have had much evidence of the Western Governments' very palpable reluctance to use nuclear weapons against Korean-type aggression, and risk precipitating a general war.

So there would be little risk of encouraging such aggression if we adopted and announced a policy of graduated action, while this would emphasise that we are more disposed to take a firm line. At the same time the will to resist would be strengthened among the peoples on our side if they were made aware that there was a hopeful intermediate policy of checking aggression in a non-suicidal way. A public announcement would be the most effective way to make them aware of it.

To evolve a workable plan of graduated action is certainly a knotty problem, requiring extensive study, yet at least worth trying as an alternative to world suicide.

The best chance would obviously lie in confining nuclear weapons to the immediate battlefield, and the chances would decrease in each successive stage of deeper use. At the same time, even the second stage in depth—their use against the the aggressor's Lines of Communication area, and his airfields there—would involve a heavy additional handicap, since the British and American forces will be operating overseas and their seaport advanced bases will be more vulnerable than the other side's land communications.

So there would be compensating advantages for the Western Powers in confining nuclear action to the battlefield—which is also the most practicable differential, and perhaps the only one that will allow the defence a chance of profiting by unconventional weapons without precipitating an all-out war. One can, however, see possible ways in which a land-based attacker of strategic ingenuity might nullify a defence geared to tactical atomic weapons—which depend for effect on suitable targets, and are ineffective against dispersion or intermingling.

Is there any other way of increasing our defensive strength, and with a greater chance of avoiding all-out nuclear warfare?

A better prospect of limitation is offered by the use of chemical instead of nuclear weapons. For chemical weapons are most effective in checking invasion and delaying all advancing movements on land, while far less effective against stationary forces and cities. It is absurd to forego the defensive use of mustard gas, the most obstructive yet least lethal of weapons, while adopting the use of nuclear weapons—which are weapons of mass-slaughter, and violate the lawful code of warfare on more counts than such a weapon as mustard gas, which is relatively humane. The ban has become still more nonsensical since the development of non-lethal nerve gases which annul the will to fight.

But the safest course of all in defence would be to rely on conventional forces using purely conventional weapons. This possibility is examined in later chapters.

THE NEW PROBLEM OF " LIMITED WAR " STRATEGY

It is essential to realise that while the H-bomb has become a check on the deliberate launching of an all-out attack, it has not reduced the possibilities of limited war to the same extent, and may even increase them. In this kind of operation a subtle strategist can develop a variety of techniques, different in pattern but all aimed to gain aggressive objectives while causing hesitancy on the other side in taking the fateful decision to order counteraction with nuclear weapons. To repeat but amplify my earlier definition—

Such aggression might be made at a limited tempo—a gradual process of encroachment.

It might be made at a fast tempo but to a limited depth—small blitz bites swiftly made, and as swiftly followed up by a conciliatory offer to negotiate.

It might take the form of stirring up internal revolt in another country, and then infiltrating or parachuting reinforcements of volunteers.

It might also take a purely subversive form.

It is ironical that the more the Western Powers have developed the massiveness of their strategic air force and the explosive force of the nuclear weapon the more they have tended to aid the progress of the new " mosquito " type strategy employed against them. Their own strategy should be based on a clear grasp of this concept, and their military policy should be adjusted to fit it.

THE SOLUTION PROPOSED

What should be done to meet such a wide variety of dangers, ranging from total war to cold war? Can it be done without incurring a financial burden that will break us without a battle?

The maintenance and improvement of the nuclear deterrent to war, especially to all-out war, remains the primary requirement.

But there is no need for a strategic bombing force of great size—as in the last war. With H-bombs, only a small number suffice to inflict overwhelming destruction, if they reach their target. So what counts is not quantity of bombers, but superlative technical *quality* and performance. That applies also to the long-range missile which is superseding the bomber as the means of delivery. There is all the less need for quantity since the purpose is to prevent war, by deterring a would-be

63

attacker, and not to pursue the now futile and obsolete aim of winning a war.

Once NATO learns with wisdom of concentrating on deterrence, instead of out-of-date preparation for waging a great war, great savings can be made in bombing forces of the customary kind. For air defence, fighter forces add little to the deterrent compared with their cost, and would be of little avail. They can be scrapped now—except such part of them as is required for co-operation with troops in " small " warfare—instead of waiting until the new missile-type air defence is ready.

In all services, too, large savings can be made by cutting out preparations and stock-piling for a long war of the old unlimited kind.

We can turn now to what is required to meet the local and limited types of aggression that form the most likely risk— frontier " bites ", quick or gradual, and internal outbreaks fomented from outside. To tackle these, the need is for an extensive gendarmerie backed by mobile forces of high efficiency, in a state of constant readiness—like fire brigades. A short-service conscript Army is badly fitted for such tasks; a relatively small professional Army would be much better. It could be usefully supplemented, however, by a superior militia type force, locally based.

In tackling these small war emergencies we have got to reckon with the possibility that, if the " fire " is not quickly quenched, it may spread—and develop, unintended by either side, into an all-out war. So tactics, movement, formations and organisations must always be adaptable to the possibility that nuclear weapons may suddenly be used.

In this new model Army, which I visualise, the active troops might be of two types. The striking element would consist of a number of handy-sized armoured divisions, mounted entirely in cross-country vehicles that can move off the road. They would be trained to operate in controlled dispersion like a swarm of hornets, offering little target to a nuclear bomb or missile if such were used.

The other type, for policing and for mobile defence, would be "light infantry" divisions. They would also be completely capable of moving off roads—but not through mechanisation. Their cross-country capacity would come from lightness of equipment. They would be armed mainly with light weapons that a man can carry, and only such supporting weapons as can be carried on a mule—or the new Italian type mechanised mule—and do not require a heavy load of ammunition. Where necessary, but only where necessary, a regiment of self-propelled guns could be attached to them, and likewise a regiment of light tanks or cross-country armoured cars.

Besides these mobile forces, it would also be a good insurance—especially against the new risk of a conventional type invasion—if the Continental countries were to create militia-type forces—organised to fight in their own locality and maintain themselves from local stores, distributed in numerous small underground shelters. Such forces, a superior form of Home Guard, would provide a deep network of defence, yet need much less transport than the present NATO type, be much less of a target, be less liable to interception, and become effective with far shorter training—so relieving the present burden of conscription. Blended with a stronger gendarmerie, similarly localised, they would also be better offensively and defensively for guerrilla-like warfare.

Part of those in rearward areas might be moved up as reinforcements to the forward layers of the defence if, and as, conditions allowed. With suitable planning, that could be done—without these forces needing the large scale of organic transport and equipment that makes the existing NATO type divisions so vulnerable, as well as so costly.

65

Such a reorganisation would provide the NATO countries with a chance of effective defence without the extreme peril of resorting to nuclear weapons—and thus strengthen the deterrent. For the prime need today is to reinforce the H-bomb deterrent, which has turned into a two-edged threat, by developing a non-nuclear fireguard and fire-extinguisher —on the ground, and ready for use without hesitation or delay.

THE NEW DEVELOPMENT OF STRATEGY

Old concepts, and old definitions, of strategy have become *not only obsolete*, but *nonsensical* with the development of nuclear weapons. The development of long-range rockets, to replace the manned bomber aircraft, makes the absurdity even clearer.

To aim at winning a war, to take victory as your object, is no more than a state of lunacy. For a total war, with nuclear weapons, would be fatal to both sides.

There is no sense even in planning for such a war—for a World War III, as it is often called. In the present state of scientific development, the destruction and chaos would be so great *within a few hours* that the war could not continue in any *organised* sense.

Yet it is astonishing to see the extent to which old-fashioned concepts continue to influence military planning. They are repeatedly revealed by the use of out-of-date terms, and the pattern of exercises. This is shown even in the use of the word " sword " for the deterrent—which is mainly provided by the U.S. strategic air force—and " shield " for the NATO ground forces. For the sword could not be *used*, actually, without producing *mutual suicide*. It is like the old ceremonial Japanese sword dedicated for committing *hara-kiri*. And the old word shield does not suggest the kind of protection required to meet the nibbling, erosive forms of aggression that have now become more likely than sword-thrusts. A shield is not a suitable protection against wasps, nor against incendiary fires.

Strategy—which aims at military victory—should always be subordinate to Grand Strategy, the realm of statesmanship which is concerned with the ultimate state of peace. This has too often been disregarded in the past. Now, more than ever Grand Strategy must be in the driving seat.

Statesmanship, in the H-bomb age, must control not only the aims but the operations. It should direct military defence planning, and the formulation of military doctrine. Hence statesmen and their diplomatic advisers must have a greater knowledge of military technique than they needed in the past. That is as important as for soldiers to submit to political direction. Even if we do not go so far as to merge the function of the Foreign Minister and the Defence Minister, they and their expert advisers must combine much more closely.

It is a new version of Plato's dictum that the affairs of the world would not improve until either the philosophers became the rulers or the rulers became philosophers.

6

THE PERILS OF H-TRIGGER ALERTNESS

IT is curious how slow people have been in awakening to the new and tremendously increased risks of our situation. It is even more curious how their awakening has begun in an indirect way, from startling sidelights.

London and the other great cities of Western Europe have been within the range of Russian rockets for a long time past —since 1955 at least—yet it was only the launching of the Sputnik that made the Western peoples conscious of the danger under which they lie from rocket bombardment. Even the military chiefs who had full information of the radar-traced flights of Russian rockets did not really believe that the Russians had outstripped them in missile development, and went on assuming that the West had a great superiority in bombardment power, until the Sputnik shook them out of their customary and comfortable assumption.

Slow to grow, too, has been a realisation of the fast-growing risk that a great disaster may arise *accidentally*—from the intense efforts which are being made to attain instant readiness for nuclear retaliation. Even now hardly anybody realises what an immense, and acute, risk it has become.

Public and parliamentary anxiety in Britain about the risk started from a casually disclosed sidelight in November 1957. The commander of the United States Strategic Air Command, General Power (a too apt name) then mentioned during a visit to Paris that since the beginning of October his force—

which totals over 2,000 jet bombers—had been put in such a state of readiness that one-third of it could get into the air within fifteen minutes' warning. He went on to say that the aircraft, with bombs on board, were kept at the end of their runways, with the crews sleeping beside them. He also said that a proportion were kept always in the air, day and night.

In the House of Commons Mr. Frank Allaun called attention to this statement and the danger it implied. Mr. Aneurin Bevan then asked the Secretary of State for Foreign Affairs whether " American aircraft on patrol from the American bases in Britain carry hydrogen bombs ". Mr. Selwyn Lloyd replied in a guarded way, saying " it may very well be so". When pressed, he said that he was " prepared to assume " that the aircraft actually carried H-bombs.

Mr. Selwyn Lloyd also said that if there was an accident to the aircraft there would be no danger of the nuclear weapon exploding. But atomic scientists then pointed out that if an aircraft carrying the bomb were to crash there would be serious danger of radioactive and highly poisonous, material being scattered over the area. The Prime Minister, Mr. Harold Macmillan, subsequently admitted this risk although he went on to describe it as " a small risk ". That would carry more conviction as a reassurance if it were not a habit of governments, in all countries, to minimise uncomfortable facts. But the risk of death-spreading radiation from such a possible crash is, even at its greatest, small compared with another risk of patrols and practice flights by loaded H-bombers. For a misinterpretation of code signals by aircraft thus loaded might all too easily lead to the starting of nuclear war—and thereby to the almost instantaneous destruction of civilisation.

The likelihood of such a fatal accident has been much increased by efforts to quicken the bombing forces' readiness for retaliatory action, in order to shorten the time of take-off and despatch with their bomb-loads. It could happen all too quickly in a period of acute tension and international crisis!

General Power's disclosure that a large proportion of the bombers can take off at fifteen minutes' notice with their devastating loads, and that part of them are always in the air, was a clear indication of how far the whole process of acceleration has been carried. Moreover, the risk of accident, and particularly through overstretched nerves, naturally becomes multiplied when intermediate commanders and bomber crews are kept in such a keyed-up state. Even a single crew, if it fused its H-bomb when on patrol and delivered this to a target in Russia's sphere, or the other way round, might start a chain reaction that could wreck the world within a few hours.

It is extremely difficult to devise precautions against misinterpretation or misuse of code orders that are compatible with quick action. The quicker the action required, and aimed at, the more difficult any adequate precautions become.

Even in the more leisurely days of the past there were some startling examples of what a misused or misinterpreted codeword could set going. I was strongly impressed with this possibility by a small case in World War I that I witnessed myself —when a commander, after a heavy drinking bout, sent out the codeword for invasion. The machinery for an emergency entrainment and move to the East Coast had just previously been speeded up, and by the time that the misuse of the codeword was discovered, a few hours later, it had gone so far as to be difficult to stop.

A much more widely known case, in World War II, was when the codeword " Cromwell " for special alertness was sent out by G.H.Q. Home Forces on the night of September

70

7, 1940, and mistakenly interpreted in some cases to mean that an invasion had actually taken place. So church bells were rung, bridges destroyed, roads blocked, and mines precipitately laid on the roads—causing a number of fatal casualties.

A much worse " accident " was the bombing of Rotterdam on May 14, 1940. The German troops had met such stiff resistance in trying to occupy the city that a bombing attack was arranged to aid them. At midday the German general in command of the ground forces heard that a Dutch surrender was likely, and immediately signalled orders both by wireless and red flares—as a double check—to put off the bombing attack. One of the two columns of the bombing force promptly turned away, but the other either missed the signals or ignored them, and carried out the original orders. Its bombs started a swift-spreading fire which wiped out the centre of this city, destroying 20,000 buildings.

In the H-bomb era in which we live now, miscarriage or disregard of signals to bombers in the air would have immensely worse consequences. To live under the shadow of a foreign dictator's power to threaten us with H-bomb attack is perilous enough. But it is far more perilous to live under the shadow of a multiplicity of H-bombing airmen, on either side, who are keyed up to an extreme pitch of alertness, and some of whom may be feeling intensely bellicose and " trigger-happy ".

Beyond the risk of genuine misinterpretation of code signals is the risk of intentional misinterpretation. Impatient subordinate commanders have often turned a Nelson-like blind eye to restraining orders—and it has happened much more often than history records.

Mr. Macmillan in a broadcast remarked: " If occasional flights with hydrogen bombs are necessary to ensure the reliability of our defences, we must accept that necessity.

Effective deterrence depends on instant readiness to deter."
He went on to say reassuringly—

To make the bombs effective requires an elaborate piece of technical
drill by the crew of the aircraft.
None of these bombs could be, or would be used except by deliberate
military order, given upon the instruction of the British and American
Governments acting in agreement.
We ourselves have an absolute veto on the dropping of these bombs
from any plane based in this country.

Unhappily, such a top-level veto is not, and cannot be, a
convincing reassurance if the crew of an aricraft can themselves make the bomb effective and if there is no infallible
technical means of preventing them from fusing it and dropping it. Mr. Macmillan did not suggest that there is any such
technical preventive device, and his omission to say anything
on this crucial matter is in itself ominously significant.

Instant readiness for action is only possible if the bombs
are widely distributed and the actual *operative* control of
them decentralised as far as possible. But the further this
militarily necessary process is carried, the greater becomes
the risk of their fatal misuse by accident. At a time of crisis,
when passions are inflamed, a world catastrophe might be
precipitated by some intermediate commander, and even by
a bomber-crew, who felt that the heads of the government,
or Allied Governments were " selling the pass " by cravenly
pursuing appeasement.

Fatal action might also be produced by a mistaken belief
that hostile aircraft carrying H-bombs are on their way to
deliver a surprise attack on some American base or bases.
That risk becomes much greater with the advent of missiles
that reduce the time of flight and warning to a matter of
minutes. According to Washington reports, the fear of such
a Pearl Harbor stroke has led the U.S. Government to
authorise local commanders to unleash their own nuclear

weapons if they believe that their bases are in imminent peril of destruction. Such " conditional advance consent " goes far to nullify the possibility of effective control by governments. The statesmen's talk of retaining an absolute veto sounds unrealistic.

It is hardly possible to frame, or rely upon, any technical safeguard that can be foolproof or governmental check that can be effective when detection systems can provide barely fifteen minutes' warning of a missile attack launched against the United States, and of four minutes at the most in the case of Britain and the countries in western Europe.

7

ARE SMALL ATOMIC WEAPONS
THE ANSWER?

The whole problem of defence is affected by the recent development of small-yield atomic weapons. Potentially, they change the problem—and, more certainly, complicate it. It is claimed that they will bring about a fresh revolution in warfare—of different effect from that caused by the advent of the atomic bomb in 1945—by enabling nuclear weapons to be used without bringing on all-out war, thus enhancing deterrence by combining it with effective defence.

Until 1945, the most powerful bomb produced was less than ten tons. The bomb then dropped on Hiroshima had an explosive force nearly two thousand times as great. It created an immense gulf between atomic and what are called conventional weapons. Then came another enormous jump in destructiveness with the development of the hydrogen bomb in 1954—a thousand-fold multiplication of the power of the original atomic bomb.

But now the latest developments have gone in the opposite direction—towards producing atomic weapons of very small size and very limited explosive force. For among the nuclear weapons tested in the Nevada desert in 1958 were seven that had an explosive yield of less than one hundred tons. One of them had an explosive yield of only thirty-six tons, and another only six tons—less than that of the ordinary large bomb dropped by aircraft in the later part of World War II. Weapons with a yield of less than one ton are on the horizon.

Are Small Atomic Weapons the Answer?

Why are such small-yield atomic weapons being developed, and what are the particular advantages claimed for them ? The first is that they turn the military use of nuclear power from a blind means of " mass destruction " into a weapon of precision and discrimination. They can be used tactically, by troops in battle, without devastating the towns and cities in the area where they are employed. That is potentially a great gain in humanity and benefit to civilisation. It is also a safeguard to the morale of the people of the country for whose defence they are used. Small nations are more likely to be firm in resisting enemy threats and aggression if they feel that there is a good chance of invasion being repelled without having their homeland devastated in the process of defence.

From the military point of view, there is also a great advantage in the prospect of being able to produce as much killing effect, and destructive effect on fortified defences, with a single artillery piece as has hitherto required scores or hundreds of guns. Moreover, the effect of even a very small nuclear burst is so much greater than any ordinary shell-burst that a single shot may achieve more, both materially and morally, than a prolonged bombardment or barrage of the normal kind—which calls for a lavish and continuous supply of ammunition.

Thus there could be a very great economy, by reduction, in the quantity of guns, of ammunition, of transport vehicles to carry the ammunition, and of fuel to move the transport vehicles—as well as of shipping, in the case of military forces that have to be sent, and maintained, overseas.

Such a great reduction in weapon and supply needs would go far to simplify and diminish the logistical problems of armies—which have been causing an increasingly heavy headache to military planners. The " tail " of an army could become very small compared with its present bulk, as the

75

need for large ammunition dumps and depots for their supply, which form extensive targets, would be eliminated.

At first sight it would also appear that the " teeth " as well as the tail would be much less vulnerable than at present. For a handful of nuclear-firing guns, well distributed, would be a very slight target compared with a mass of batteries firing ordinary shells. On the other hand, a reduction in the number of weapons on which an army depends tends to make its weapon system vulnerable in a different way. For numbers are an important factor in any calculation of vulnerability. If there are fewer targets for the enemy to attack, the effect of a successful attack on a small number of them is apt to be much greater. Moreover, nuclear-firing guns are very vulnerable because, once they have fired, it is comparatively easy for the enemy to locate and destroy them. That also applies to liquid-fuelled guided weapons or missiles, as these take a considerable time to prepare for firing.

Tactically, the prospective advantages of small-yield atomic weapons are that they allow much more discrimination, that they enable acceleration of action in engaging targets, that they can be profitably used against much smaller targets, and—what is most important—can be employed much closer to one's own troops than has been possible with the large tactical atomic weapons of the 10–20 kiloton range hitherto in vogue.

There is a great tactical advantage in being able to fire at enemy troops until they are within a few hundred yards of one's own, compared with the drawback of having to cease fire when the enemy are a mile or more away. For if there is such a wide stretch of " dead ground "—i.e. ground against which nuclear weapons cannot be used—an attacker may be able to arrive there by stealthy and dispersed approach, and then have a good chance of assembling sufficient strength, in this " nuclear-safe " belt, to break into the defence. Once he has broken in, it would hardly be possible for the defending forces to use large-yield tactical atomic weapons to stop his continued penetration of the area they themselves are occupying.

Moreover, present means and methods of locating and engaging targets suitable for large-yield nuclear weapons are apt to be much too slow to catch them before they disappear. At night the difficulty is still worse. But these means and methods of what is called " target acquisition " would have a better chance with small-yield weapons employed at close range.

With the present tactical atomic weapons, of 10 to 20 kilotons, it would hardly be worth while to use them against targets smaller than a brigade or regimental group. But with the small-yield weapons now in prospect, units as small as a platoon might become atomic targets. The Americans have already got atomic warheads as small as five inches in diameter, and have developed infantry mortars that can fire atomic shells, and are easily handled by a few men.

What are the disadvantages of the development of such small-yield atomic weapons? In the first place, they are a very uneconomic form of nuclear power, as such limited explosive yield is only possible through using fissile material as inefficiently as possible. That technical disadvantage may be offset by the tactical and logistical advantages, as well as by wider considerations. It is argued that these promise an economy of force that outweighs the technically uneconomic process of producing small-yield atomic weapons.

But the argument becomes dubious when set against the limits of a country's defence budget and productive effort, together with the fact that it is as easy, and in some ways easier, to produce the larger-yield warheads. It is a mistake to assume that a much larger number of the small-yield warheads can be produced from a given amount of fissile material, effort and money. These limiting conditions cast doubt on the optimistic view of their advocates that small targets, down to a platoon, will become worth-while targets.

Moreover, the advantages promised would only be attainable if armies, and Governments, decide to take the risk of discarding most of their present equipment in conventional weapons, and relying on a relatively small quantity of small-yield atomic weapons as a substitute.

The boldness of such a step is an inherent hindrance to such a decision. Once taken, it might not fit the circumstances, yet would be irretrievable. Although guns and mortars, as well as rocket-launchers, may have *dual capacity* —to fire either nuclear or conventional projectiles—the number of pieces that would suffice to provide a shattering bombardment with atomic shells would be utterly inadequate when firing ordinary high explosive shells. It would be like changing from a fireman's hose to a garden sprinkler. But if the number was to be adequate for the needs of conventional fighting, the economy would be forfeited.

Another drawback is the uncertainty of what will be the effect on one's own troops of turning a conventional into a nuclear fight. It might prove a boomerang, shaking their nerve by the frightfulness of the experience, and leading to a moral collapse.

This brings us to another big question which applies to tactical atomic weapons in general. The main argument for equipping the NATO forces with such weapons has been that they are essential to counterbalance the Soviet Army's much larger number of troops. This argument is based on the belief that tactical atomic weapons favour the defence, and on the view that an attacker must concentrate his forces if he is to succeed in breaking through the defence, thereby offering packed targets to the defender's atomic weapons. Is this true?

The presence of atomic weapons certainly reduces the number of troops that an attacker can safely deploy in an area. But that limitation also applies to the defender—reducing the number of troops he can safely position in the area. That condition in turn affects the prevailing NATO belief and view. For the more the defence is dispersed over a given space, the less the attacker needs to concentrate his forces in order to penetrate the defence.

Indeed, his prospects may in this respect become better than they have been previously, before the advent of nuclear weapons. For where the defence ratio of force to space falls below the minimum required for a closely woven network of fire, a skilful attacker has always had a better chance of success, and required a lower ratio of superiority in strength to overcome the defence. Dispersion inherently increases the scope for flank-turning manoeuvre, internal or external.

This basic condition applies to operations where tactical atomic weapons are used, or may be used—enforcing mutual dispersion. When tactical atomic weapons were first developed, I came to the conclusion, after a study of the problem, that it was very doubtful whether they would favour the defending side, as was claimed. Indeed I thought out a method of " busting " a defence based on the type and scale of tactical atomic weapons then visualised (i.e. in the 20 kiloton range) which seemed to me to offer as good prospects to a skilful attacker as the mechanised " expanding torrent " attack originally did when conceived before the last war.

The question remains how far this conclusion will be affected by the development of very low-yield tactical atomic weapons. Because of their much reduced radius of destructive effect, they can be used in a more discriminating way, and with less risk to the defender's own troops—thus reducing the dead ground area in which an attacker could concentrate at the last moment, after a dispersed approach. That should favour the defence. On the other hand the increased dispersion enforced on the defender diminishes the attacker's need to concentrate—enabling a dispersed attacking force to infiltrate more easily. And once it had infiltrated into the defender's position, it exerts the moral effect characteristic of any threat to the defender's rear, which tends to be largely an effective substitute for physical weight and effect.

In arguing that tactical atomic weapons give an advantage to the defence in general, and NATO's defence in particular, the most that can reasonably be claimed is that their presence tends to be a check on the attacker concentrating a very large *quantitative* superiority. Even if he has an overall superiority of 3 to 1 he could hardly venture to mass enough troops in any particular area to produce a local superiority of 10 to 1, or even 5 to 1, at the intended point of breakthrough. On the other hand, since the presence of atomic weapons enforces dispersion on both sides the attacker may have a better chance than hitherto of achieving *qualitative* advantage by superior tactical skill. It may even enable him to break through without any numerical superiority.

Thus, in sum and on balance, it becomes very doubtful whether the equipment of the NATO forces with tactical atomic weapons carries benefits comparable to its added risks. Even the potential advantages of the small-yield type, which appear so good at first sight, tend to fade in the light of closer examination.

A wider consideration is that the control of small-yield atomic weapons will be much more decentralised, especially when infantry battalions are equipped with mortars which can fire them. That reduces the check upon their unpremeditated use in a local emergency. They could so easily be loosed off.

Are Small Atomic Weapons the Answer?

In theory, these small-yield weapons offer a better chance of confining nuclear action to the battle-zone, and thus limiting its scale and scope of destructiveness—to the benefit of humanity and the preservation of civilisation. But once any kind of nuclear weapon is actually used, it could all too easily spread by rapid degrees, and lead to all-out nuclear war. The lessons of experience about the emotional impulses of men at war are much less comforting than the theory—the tactical theory which has led to the development of these weapons.

8

IS GAS A BETTER ALTERNATIVE ?

WESTERN Defence has become increasingly based upon, and thus committed to, the employment of tactical atomic weapons—a commitment developing from the 1954 decision to equip the forces, ground and air, with weapons of this kind.

But since then the Russians, too, have developed tactical atomic weapons. So it is no longer possible to count on the NATO equipment of this kind as a counterbalance to the Russians' superior numbers. It is also very doubtful whether tactical atomic weapons favour the defence more than the attack.

At the same time it is known that the Russian troops are highly trained for operating under atomic battle conditions, especially in skilful use of dispersion and darkness. Indeed, they may be better trained for this " game " than most of the NATO troops.

Moreover, the military heads of NATO have never shown any confidence that atomic action can be limited, and confined to the tactical field. On the contrary, they have often conveyed the impression that once such weapons are unleashed, their use will soon spread into all-out nuclear war —which means mutual suicide and world destruction.

General Gruenther, then the Supreme Commander, expressed that view even in 1954, when the decision was taken to introduce tactical atomic weapons. So did Field-Marshal Montgomery. That same gloomy conclusion was reiterated in 1957 by Gruenther's successor, General Norstad, who said that in his own mind he found it impossible to draw a line between the tactical use of such weapons, against an attacker's forces, and their strategical use, against the homelands.

The conclusion was re-emphasised, with greater force, in 1958 by Admiral Charles R. Brown, the present Commander-in-Chief of the Allied Forces, Southern Europe. Speaking in Washington, just before taking over this high command, he said: " I have no faith in the so-called controlled use of atomic weapons. There is no dependable distinction between tactical and strategic situations. I would not recommend the use of any atomic weapon, no matter how small, when both sides have the power to destroy the world." His conclusion was the more significant because of his study of the problem in his previous post as Commander of the U.S. Sixth Fleet in the Mediterranean—the most powerful striking force in Europe and the Near East.

Is there any better, and more hopeful, alternative in sight as an effective but non-suicidal means of defence?

Gas offers such an alternative—especially in the new disabling but non-lethal forms that have been developed. Even in World War I the most effective chemical weapon was mustard gas, which disabled more but killed fewer than any other important weapon. Moreover it favoured, and aided, defence by its obstructive and delaying effect.

Now, new gases have been developed which are far more paralysing as an antidote to aggression. They can " make a cat frightened of a mouse "—not only in the metaphorical, but in the literal sense of the phrase.

This development fulfils a vision of nearly forty years ago. Soon after the First World War, I argued, in a little book on *The Future of War*, that " self-interest as well as humane reasons demand that warring nations should endeavour to gain their end . . . with the least possible permanent injury to life and industry. To inflict widespread death and destruction is to damage one's own future property, and, by sowing the seeds of revenge, to jeopardise one's future security ". I went on to suggest that: " Chemical science has provided mankind with a weapon which reduces the necessity of killing and achieves decisive effects with far less permanent injury than in the case of explosives."

Ironically, this hopeful prospect was hindered by the solemn prohibition of the use of gas in warfare which was formulated and agreed at the Washington Conference of 1921, and subsequently repeated at Geneva. The signatory Powers at Washington added to the prohibition an undertaking " to denounce the use of poisonous gases and chemicals in war, as they were used to the horror of all civilisation in the war of 1914–18".

That denunciation was an emotional revulsion, particularly against a novelty in weapons, rather than a reasoned conclusion from the facts of war experience. Its irrationality became evident in analysis of the casualty figures—of which full and classified details were compiled for the British and American armies. Among the British casualties from bullets or high explosive shells, the proportion was approximately one dead out of every three men hit, whereas among the gas casualties only one man in thirty died.

The American figures were even more illuminating. Coming into the war at a late stage, their army met gas warfare at its peak, and nearly one-third of their total casualties were caused by gas. But only one in fifty died compared with one in four of those caused by bullets or high explosive shells. Thus a soldier disabled by gas had twelve times as much chance of recovery.

The difference between the British and American ratios is explained by the fact that the British suffered the chlorine gas attacks of 1915 and the even more deadly but less pain-causing phosgene gas in 1916, whereas by the time the Americans arrived on the battlefield these types had been largely superseded by mustard gas, which was more effective but less lethal, even though painful.

In the first gas attack, in April 1915, the French and British troops at Ypres were taken unawares, and the sight of men choking to death as the greenish-yellow mist spread over their trenches produced a feeling of terror and horror—which was vastly multiplied by sensational reporting, and subsequent propaganda. In these first attacks, too, the death-roll was nearly one in four of those affected. A novel weapon that caused almost as high a proportion of deaths as the conventional bullet or shell naturally appeared more barbarous. That first impression, and its exploitation by propaganda, obscured from the public mind the much-diminished lethalness in proportion to disabling effectiveness of the improved gases that were employed later in the war.

Yet a clear deduction from the death ratios among casualties was that poison gas as used in World War I was far more humane as a weapon than shells, bombs, or even bullets. That applied even to the more painful forms of gas—for most men would prefer a period of pain to a ten-times greater chance of death. Moreover, the relative humaneness of the chemical weapon was all the greater because the military effect could be, and was, achieved without the destruction of towns and devastation of countries inevitably produced by explosive weapons.

Thus the main effect of the Washington and Geneva prohibition of gas was, ironically and tragically, to preserve for the battlefields of the future the more fatal effects of high explosive, and also its shattering effects on the structure of civilised society. For explosive weapons destroy the economic foundations of a return from war to peace. Once the conductors of war were left without an alternative kind of weapon, that danger was bound to increase as air-power developed—and would be immensely multiplied by the development of atomic power.

Although research and experiment with gases continued, the signed agreement to prohibit their use in war became a restraint on military study of the tactical use of gas and the practice of it in troop exercises. No army liked to appear to be preparing to employ gas in war.

Such restraint was reinforced by the soldierly dislike of unconventional weapons that has always been prevalent. It was typified in ancient times by the Spartan commander Archidamus, who, on seeing a dart shot from a new catapult-machine, exclaimed " O Hercules, the valour of man is at an end ". In the same spirit the Chevalier Bayard, the model of mediaeval chivalry, showed no mercy to musketeers, in contrast to his kindly treatment of captured swordsmen and pikemen.

There was also a soldierly distrust of the value of non-lethal gases. That was typified by the response made by a general concerned with such weapons to the British chemist who suggested the use of dichlorethyl-sulphide (mustard gas) —two years before the Germans adopted it. The general's immediate question was: " Does it kill?" The chemist replied: " No, but it will disable enormous numbers of the enemy temporarily "—whereat the general said: " That is no good to us; we want something that will kill."

Such soldierly dislike and distrust of chemical weapons, coupled with lack of familiarity and practice with them between the wars, were influential factors in preventing the use of them in World War II—as influential, probably, as the deterrent knowledge that both sides possessed and could use them in retaliation if they were re-introduced. In a similar way, the C.D.L. tanks (fitted with special flicker searchlights for blinding the enemy as well as night-firing), a British invention on which many million pounds were spent, were never used in the war—having been kept so secret that the commanders in the field regarded them distrustfully and thus repeatedly hesitated to employ such unfamiliar instruments.

If the Western Allies had used mustard gas in 1940 they could almost certainly have stopped the Germans from breaking through the Meuse front and overrunning France. For even if the tanks could have driven on, the foot-marching infantry masses could not have followed to back them up, and they would have been left isolated. Thus France could have been saved from defeat. In 1944–45, too, the Germans could have held up the Allies' land advance by the same means, even though they might still have succumbed to the Allies' overwhelming air attack.

That reflection casts doubt on the oft-repeated assertion that, in an emergency, nations will use any means to save themselves from defeat, and to win the war, regardless of any rules of war to which they have agreed in peacetime. Unfamiliarity with a weapon, and uncertainty about its results, have as much restraining power as any treaty promise.

But in the limitation of war, the restraint on the use of gas that followed its formal prohibition and practical discard after World War I has not proved to the advantage of humanity and civilisation. The development of explosives continued apace, led on to the atomic bomb, and culminated in the hydrogen (thermo-nuclear) bomb—which now threatens world-destruction. Moreover, countries which may be invaded nowadays by an aggressor with numerically superior forces, using conventional weapons, are faced with the grim choice between the certainty of defeat, which spells enslavement, and the near certainty of suicide, if nuclear weapons are used in their defence.

A reversion to chemical weapons would at least offer a

better alternative, and more hope of successful defence without suicide—if deterrence fails. Chemical weapons are most effective in checking invasion and delaying all advancing movements on land, whereas they are far less effective against stationary forces and cities. By the end of World War II, new gases were developed that could penetrate any advancing tanks and knock out their crews within a fraction of a minute. While mustard gas is not so decisive as an attack-quencher, it has immense disabling and delaying power, and remains supremely effective in the latter respect.

It is particularly absurd to forego the defensive use of mustard gas, the most obstructive yet least lethal of weapons, while adopting the use of nuclear weapons—which are weapons of mass-slaughter, and violate the lawful code of warfare on more counts than such a weapon as mustard gas, which is relatively humane.

Moreover, the latest types of nerve=gas now developed are much more effective still in producing a short-term disablement of the attackers, without killing. They paralyse the will to fight, and quench the valour of the fiercest attacker.

Their effect is most striking, and, laughably, demonstrated by putting a mouse into a box along with a cat. The cat promptly pounces on the mouse—but, after a whiff of the new gas, has its instincts reversed. Every time the mouse approached, the cat jumps back in fright—even falling over backwards in its efforts to avoid the mouse! Such a demonstration, and such a gas, provide a far more hopeful portent for peace and humanity than the multiplication of the atomic deterrent.

9

COULD CONVENTIONAL FORCES
SUFFICE ?

THE Russian rocket has brought NATO round the circle to where it started in 1949—the need for a " conventional " defence and deterrent. But with a difference. For, under the ever-present shadow of nuclear war, a sudden local coup is more likely to be attempted than a mass invasion.

To provide an adequate counter to such a coup in Europe is not nearly as big a problem as is apt to be assumed—by those who still consider the problem in the old terms of defence.

Even on the old basis—of capacity to meet a full-scale invasion by the Soviet armies—the Western planners came to the conclusion, in 1950–51, that a Covering Force of thirty-four divisions—eighteen ready for immediate action—should suffice to check a surprise assault on the front between Austria and the Baltic.

While the NATO plan for this central front was subsequently expanded in 1952, to a target of twice that number, the doubling was to be mainly in the form of reserve divisions that could be mobilised to match the corresponding mobilisation of the Russian reserves. In other words, the expanded plan was a product of the customary picture of a lengthy struggle in the old style.

In the light of experience, the planners reckoned that a Covering Force of thirty-four active divisions had a good prospect of checking an attack by sixty to seventy Soviet divisions—the maximum that seemed possible, on movement and supply calculations, in the initial stage of a war. They also reckoned that, whatever the number of reinforcements which might be mobilised on the Soviet side, it would be difficult to utilise more than double that total, if as many, in a long-distance advance westward. So a NATO Covering Force and reinforcement of the scale projected in 1950–51 was considered a good insurance.

The actual build-up of the NATO forces fell far short of this planned scale—which was to have been reached by 1954. But its fulfilment was not really so impossible, militarily or economically, as is now commonly assumed.

On the NATO estimate, Russia has long maintained a standing Army of about 175 divisions, yet her total population is barely 200 million. The NATO countries have a population of 230 million in Europe, and 400 million in total, yet have produced barely twenty active divisions—of which the majority are not ready for action—to cover the western, and central, area of Europe. Indeed, the defence of this area has mainly depended on the American and British contingents, which together amount to eight divisions. The extreme disparity of ground forces is not due to disparity of available manpower, so must be due basically to deficiency of will or defective organisation. Neither is impossible to remedy.

In view of the number of divisions that Russia has been able to maintain, the question arises whether the NATO type and its supporting structure are excessively elaborate and expensive. Given the will, and new thought, the answer could be found. It makes no sense that the NATO countries should continue to live in mortal fear of a nation inferior in population and material resources, and remain impaled on the horns of a defeat or suicide dilemma.

The economic difficulties of attaining the minimum ground

strength required can be diminished by developing new tactics and organisation. The present NATO type divisions—a legacy of the last war's lavish standards—are so costly to equip that their number is restricted, so demanding in scale of supply that they would be easily paralysed in nuclear warfare, so cumbersome in scale of road transport that they are unsuited either for nuclear or guerilla conditions.

The customary type of Western division has a " tail " of non-fighting men—in the divisional service elements—more than twice as large as the Soviet tank or mechanised division, yet is weaker in firepower. The Western administrative tail, to supply and maintain the operational divisions, is larger still in proportion. Yet, basically, the defending side—operating in its own territory—should not need as high a scale of supply and transport as an attacker coming from a long distance away, and should be able to make effective defensive use of local types of force which require relatively little transport.

The prevailing view of the Western leaders that a serious invasion cannot be repelled without using nuclear weapons, and framing their plans on that basis, amounts to nothing better than a despairing acceptance of suicide in the event of any major aggression. Nothing could be more expressive of hopelessness, and more damping to the spirit of their people. These governments will be unworthy of their trust unless they tackle the problem of developing a non-suicidal form of defence and providing the minimum military strength required for it. The problem can be solved, with fresh thought and effort, at no greater cost than what is being at present spent on an illusion of defence.

It would have been better if the original NATO plan had never been abandoned. For it provided the possibility of real defence—of repelling invasion without bringing on nuclear war. A prime cause of its abandonment, apart from the zest for new gadgets, was the heavy expense of raising and equipping so many divisions. But the estimated expense was needlessly inflated by habits of thought persisting from the last war about the elaborate equipment and organisation required. If the divisions had been reorganised on a more economic pattern, and tactics also remodelled, an adequate shield force could have been produced at much less cost. The primary need was more thought, and fresh thought.

Now the problem has changed, and in the process the scale of ground forces required has diminished. For the Russians could hardly count on being able to carry out a massive invasion of long extent without precipitating a suicidal nuclear war. The most that they might hope to bring off is a sudden pounce of a limited kind, brief in time and short in extent. That is a possible venture, and danger, for which NATO should be prepared.

What strength could the Russians employ in such a pounce? There are twenty Russian divisions in East Germany, all now of mobile armoured type—eight are tank divisions and twelve are mechanised divisions. The shock force for a surprise stroke might possibly be raised to forty divisions by stealthy reinforcement without alerting the West—although an assault on that scale is the less likely because it would produce a greatly increased risk of bringing on all-out nuclear war. Nevertheless, it may be wise to reckon with the " Worst Possible Case ".

What strength does NATO need as an insurance against it? The ratio of space to force is the crux of the problem— unless the defender is low in spirit and poor in mobility compared with the opposing force. The issue tends to turn on whether the attacker has room for manoeuvre—to outflank, or penetrate weak stretches in, the opposing network of fire. Yet even on such a very wide front as that in Russia it became evident that a well-conducted mobile defence could be maintained indefinitely unless the attacking side had an *overall* superiority considerably exceeding 3 to 1. (This subject is examined more fully in the following chapter.)

It would be wise to make a larger allowance for the unequal quality of the present NATO forces—with their mixture of nationalities and of training systems—and for increased efficiency on the Russian side. Even so, they ought to be able to hold their own with a ratio of 1 to 2, while a ratio of 2 to 3 should ensure a safe margin.

On that basis, a mobile force of twenty to thirty active divisions should be a good insurance not only against a sudden pounce by the Soviet troops that are on the spot, but also against the possible but less likely scale of assault that might be achieved by stealthy reinforcement prior to the pounce. (See Chapter 16.)

Numerically, the lower insurance figure has now been attained with the formation of the first lot of German divisions, and the higher insurance figure will be within close reach when the rest of the promised twelve German divisions are formed. Thus, in terms of numbers, only a small further effort is required from the other member countries; the return of the four French divisions that were sent to Algeria would bridge the gap.

But the insurance cannot be regarded as good until the state of readiness for action is much improved. The proportion of M-day divisions is too small.

No less important is their suitability, for kinds of action that are most likely to be needed—i.e. quenching a local outbreak of " fire " before it spreads, or repelling a sudden pounce by mechanised or airborne forces. These two kinds of action call for different types of force—light infantry divisions (with a minimum of heavy equipment and road-bound transport) primarily in the first case; armoured divisions primarily in the second case. And in either case the addition of a localised militia would increase the insurance at comparatively little cost.

The customary type of heavily armed infantry division, or brigade group, which is still the preponderant element in the NATO Shield Force, is much less suitable for either of these kinds of action. The light infantry division would cost less and require less tail (of non-fighting personnel), so that more divisions could be provided from the same amount of money and manpower. That would be an aid towards making " fire-extinguishers " available for the small countries, such as Denmark, that lie on the flanks of the main, Central Europe, front—dangerously exposed to a Russian pounce. On the main front the divisions should be mainly of armoured type since the Russian divisions poised there are now all of this type.

At present the first-line forces of the Continental countries are composed of nominally active divisions constituted largely of short-term conscripts who are not fitted for quick action and mobile operations. It would be better if a large part of these Continental armies was built on a local militia basis, organised to fight in its own locality, and maintain itself from local stores, distributed in numerous small underground shelters. Such forces, a superior form of Home Guard, would provide a deep network of defence yet need much less transport than the present NATO type, be much less of a target, be less liable to interception, and become effective with far shorter training—so relieving the present burden of conscription. Blended with a stronger gendarmerie, similarly localised, they would also be better offensively and defensively for guerrilla-like warfare.

On the central front, in Germany, they should be backed by mobile forces composed of professional troops, mounted entirely in armoured cross-country vehicles, streamlined in organisation, and trained to operate in " controlled dispersion "

94

like a swarm of hornets. With such quality and mobility, fewer would be required than of present NATO divisions, while being better fitted for guerrilla-like war as well as for atomic war—wherein mobile action would only be practicable for relatively small forces. The idea that the present NATO forces are capable of fighting a mobile battle is another current illusion. It would lie with the overseas members of NATO, especially Britain and the U.S.A., to provide most of the mobile armoured forces.

In the event of nuclear weapons being used, the three types of force proposed are better suited to survive than the present " heavy " kind of infantry division.

This reflection brings us back, in conclusion, to the problem of tactical atomic weapons. It would be better if such weapons had never been introduced. Not only have they increased the risk of local conflicts developing into total war, but they may even turn to our disadvantage—now that the Russians have also got them. For besides the vulnerability of our seaport bases, static defence positions may prove more vulnerable than a well-dispersed attacking force of armoured type. There is reason to think that the Russians have gone ahead of Western armies in developing methods of dispersed and invisible advance.

But since the Russians have got the tactical atomic weapon the Western forces can hardly discard it. It is bound to be kept as " a card up the sleeve "—though we should be wiser to keep it well up the sleeve than to play it at an early stage. It should be regarded as a " last but one " resort—and it would at least be worth using it, in a limited way, before unleashing strategic nuclear action against the hinterland.

We are left with the problem of how the tactical atomic weapon can be kept without making the NATO forces so dependent on it, and their organisation so entwined with it, that they are incapable of effective action in non-nuclear ways.

To embody any form of such weapon in divisions, or even in corps, is a short-sighted policy—however attractive it may look. The best solution is to abstain from organisational integration, except at the highest levels—in other words, to allot the weapon only to special nuclear-weapon detachments that can be kept attachable, high up the sleeve.

As the use of such weapons might all too easily spread into all-out war, we need to develop a new system for higher control that will combine restraining power with rapidity, and political with military judgement in any decision to use them. It is too risky to leave the decision to military commanders. For they will always tend to use every weapon available if it looks likely that their troops will be overrun. In that immediate concern they tend to lose sight of wider issues. By taking the narrow view they have often in the past marred the aims of higher policy. Now, they could wreck the world.

In the nuclear age military strategy cannot be allowed free rein. Statesmanship ought to direct and control not only the military aim but the action, at every stage. For that purpose, new staff organs must be developed that effectively blend the two functions.

10

THE RATIO OF FORCES TO SPACE

SOME thirty years ago T. E. Lawrence—better known as Lawrence of Arabia—urged me to do a study of the ratio of force to space in war, his own conclusions being that it was of basic importance, and contained the clue to many of the puzzles of military history. In research I have been repeatedly impressed with its significance, particularly in its bearing on the prospects of attack and defence, and have been prompted to summarise and analyse the evidence on this basic matter during the last century and a half—but more particularly in the two world wars. It is a subject which ought to be much more fully explored.

One significant point which emerges from the analysis is the crucial importance of the time factor in relation to the ratio of force to space. A second is the significance of the ratio between the mobile reserves and the forces holding the front.

For at least a century and a half the number of troops needed to hold a front of any given length securely has been declining steadily. In other words, the defence has been gaining a growing material ascendancy over the offence. Even mechanised warfare has brought no radical change in this basic trend.

Looking at the experience of great armies since 1800, the first general conclusions may be drawn from the Napoleonic Wars. At that time a ratio of about 20,000 fighting troops to the mile, including reserves, was normal in holding a defensive position. That was the ratio of Wellington's five mile front at Waterloo. Two days earlier Blucher had tried to hold a seven mile front at Ligny with 12,000 to the mile and was defeated by a force slightly smaller than his own.

Fifty years later, in the American Civil War of 1861–65, the numbers had dropped substantially. During the first three years of the war a ratio of about twelve thousand fighting troops to the mile, including reserves, was normal in holding a defensive position. Later, as methods of defence developed, it was found that 5,000 men or fewer to the mile could withstand an attacker with double that strength. Lee's army held out for nine months in its long stretched line covering Richmond and Petersburg until its ratio fell below 1,500 to the mile.

The Franco-Prussian War of 1870 was decided by strategic and grand tactical manoeuvre before there could be any marked change of ratio. The figure of 12,000 to the mile was therefore normal in holding a defensive position. In the early battles, such as Gravelotte, however, the increased power of defence due to better firearms became very obvious.

In the South African War (1899–1902) the Boers—with magazine rifles and a high standard of shooting, repeatedly succeeded in repelling attacks by much larger British forces with a ratio of only 600 to 800 men to the mile. At Magersfontein the Boers had only 5,000 men on a front of six miles, and at Colenso only 4,500 men on a front of seven and a half miles.

In the Russo-Japanese War (1904–1905), a ratio of about eight thousand to the mile developed in the later and larger battles. These became protracted both in time and space. In the final great battle at Mukden, where each side had a strength of just over 300,000, the front was forty miles long, and the struggle lasted two weeks before the Japanese extending flank leverage led the Russians to retreat.

98

The Ratio of Forces to Space

WORLD WAR I, 1914–18

The First World War provides many instructive situations. After the trench deadlock developed in the autumn of 1914, the Western Front stretched from the Swiss frontier to the Channel coast—some 450 miles along the curving contour of the trench line. During 1915, when the Germans stood on the defensive in the West, they held this front with an average of ninety divisions. This was a ratio of one division for every five miles of front, or about 3,500 men to the mile. The last 100 miles at the eastern end, along the Vosges and the old fortress line, was regarded by both sides as unsuited for attack and was thus more thinly held. On the main stretch, therefore, the ratio was about one division for three miles of front (6,000 men to the mile).

The divisions actually holding the line had fronts of four to six miles in width (4,500 or 3,000 men per mile). With this ratio of troops to space, the Germans successfully repelled all the Allied attacks. Yet in the great autumn offensive of 1915 the Allies, with a total of 140 divisions (an overall superiority of three to two), managed to strike with an initial superiority averaging five to one on the sectors where they attacked.

As the war continued, both sides raised more divisions while increasing their scale of artillery support. In 1916 the Allies' strength on the Western Front was approximately 160 divisions against the Germans' 120; in 1917 it became 180 divisions against 140. But although the Allies made slightly deeper dents in the front, they failed in all attempts to break through it and generally suffered much heavier losses than the defenders.

In 1917 the Germans developed new tactics of defence, using their increased number of divisions to give it greater depth. They aimed to have a division in reserve behind each division in the line, and only one-third of each front line division was posted in the forward position. The Allies' method of long preparatory bombardment forfeited surprise and gave the Germans the chance to adjust their dispositions to meet the threat. On threatened sectors the defenders' ratio of troops to space was now often as much as one division to a mile. This was almost the Waterloo ratio of 20,000 men to a mile—although in the front line itself the ratio was only 2,000 to 3,000 men to the mile.

With the collapse of Russia in 1918, the Germans were able to bring larger reinforcements to the Western Front. They took the offensive with 190 divisions against the Allied 170, a superiority of little more than 10 per cent. By an improved technique of attack the Germans succeeded in driving deep wedges into the Allied front. But they never succeeded in pressing the exploitation far enough to achieve a complete break-through and produce a general collapse of the front.

The deepest and most dangerous penetration was in their first offensive against the British right wing in March. They drove forward forty miles in a week before being checked just short of Amiens. But there was, at this time, no adequate means of maintaining momentum in exploiting a penetration, because infantry were too slow and horse cavalry too vulnerable.

The initial success of the German break-through has been generally ascribed to the exceptional thinness of the defence on this sector, held by the British Fifth Army. But that explanation does not stand up under analysis. For the divisional fronts where the break-through occurred on March 21 were no wider than those of the Third Army at Arras, where the Germans' next heavy blow was repulsed a week later, on March 28. (On both sectors the forward divisions had fronts of about three miles apiece—which was considerably narrower than the average of the German and French.) The most significant difference in the assault conditions was the fog that cloaked the first assault, and the absence of fog when the Arras assault was launched.

But once the break-through was made the Fifth Army was handicapped in checking it by having a lower ratio of reserves than the Third Army at Arras and the two other British armies further north. There were only three divisions in reserve (apart from three cavalry divisions) behind the Fifth Army's sector of forty miles, whereas fifteen were in reserve behind the remaining eighty miles of the British front. That was the basic flaw in Haig's dispositions.

Once the German attacks of the spring and early summer had been checked, the scales of battle were decisively turned in the Allies' favour by the swelling stream of American reinforcements. Summing up the failure of the German attacks and the autumn success of the Allies, the British Official History of the campaign on the Western Front reached the conclusion that—

Even against the right wing of the Fifth Army, where the numerical superiority of the Germans was greatest, it was not sufficient to break through. . . . Armies even of the highest fighting capacity cannot make up for inadequacy of numbers by the valour of their troops or by the novelty and brilliance of their tactics; in a conflict between foes of the same standard of skill, determination and valour, numbers approaching three to one are required to turn the scale decisively, as they eventually began to do in the autumn of 1918. . . . The German efforts with insufficient numerical superiority only produced dangerous salients.

A large local superiority was often achieved during that war—even as high as 16 to 1 (by the British at Neuve Chapelle)—but there was no existing means of maintaining momentum long enough to attain a complete break-through. In the autumn of 1918 the Allies' overall superiority of 3 to 1 in fighting strength enabled them to develop a multiple leverage and push the Germans out of successive defence lines, taking large quantities of prisoners in each assault. Yet even at the time Germany was driven to appeal for an armistice, and the Allied commanders discussed its terms, Haig frankly admitted: " Germany is not broken in a military sense. During the last weeks her armies have withdrawn fighting very bravely and in excellent order. Therefore . . . it is necessary to grant Germany conditions which she can accept."

WORLD WAR II

On May 10, 1940, the Franco-British forces available to defend the 400 miles stretch of the Western Front amounted to the equivalent of 111 divisions—*a ratio of one division to three and a half miles of front.* That was a more favourable ratio of force to space than when defence prevailed over attack early in World War I. The German attack on Belgium added a further twenty-two divisions to the Allies' total, raising it to 133, without lengthening the front. Moreover, the Germans employed eight divisions in their subsidiary and divergent attack on Holland, so that their total for the offensive on the main front was reduced to 128—a total slightly less than that of the Allies.

But the Allied High Command, under Gamelin's direction, reacted and retorted to the German offensive in a way that threw its own dispositions off balance. Immediately putting into operation Plan D (which had been framed in the autumn, and dubiously accepted by the British), Gamelin rushed the Allied left wing far forward into Belgium. The force originally assigned in Plan D for this advance had been two armies (the French First and the B.E.F.), but Gamelin had recently added another (the Seventh), while using one third of the general reserve to back the advance. The total of some thirty divisions in these three armies included five of the six mechanised divisions and fifteen of the seventeen motorised divisions that the Allies possessed.

The hinge of the advance was left perilously weak—the

two armies holding the French centre having a total of only twelve divisions to hold nearly 100 miles of front facing the Ardennes. Worse still, they were mostly low-grade divisions, ill-equipped in anti-tank guns and artillery, while the front itself was poorly fortified.

Four armies were kept on the right wing behind the heavily fortified Maginot Line. Together with the garrison of the Line, and the part of the general reserve placed in this quarter, they amounted to the equivalent of more than fifty divisions. Only some ten divisions of the general reserve were actually disposable—*and they were not a mobile reserve.*

The fatal miscalculation by which the weak French centre was left exposed to attack by the strong German centre (forty-six divisions in three armies) was due—

(1)   to the Allied High Command's longstanding delusion that the Ardennes was impassable for mechanised and motorised forces.

(2)   to its confident belief that if the Germans did try to advance along that unlikely path, they would have to pause on the Meuse line to bring up heavy artillery and the mass of their infantry, and thus could not mount such an assault until the ninth or tenth day—thus allowing the Allied High Command ample time to move reserves thither, and repel the German assault when it came.

These calculations were disastrously upset—

(i)   because the Germans had recently decided to use three mechanised spearheads (comprising seven of their ten panzer divisions) in this difficult sector, as likely to be the line of least expectation.

(ii)   because these spearheads attacked the Meuse line immediately they reached it, on the fourth day (May 13), and two of the three succeeded in forcing a crossing immediately (although the German High Command itself had previously shared the Allied High Command's view that an effective assault could not be mounted until the ninth or tenth day). The principal and decisive thrust was that of Guderian's Corps of three panzer divisions at Sedan, which was supported by a massive dive-bombing attack from the Germans' much superior air forces.

Once the Meuse line was pierced and the spearheads broke out to open country, *their mechanised mobility formed the means of maintaining momentum* in exploitation, until the Channel coast was reached and the Allies' lines of supply cut—thus producing the collapse of the Allied left-wing armies, and leading on to the collapse of France.

At each stage of this exploiting drive the Allied counter-moves were ordered too late and carried out too slowly—to have a chance of saving the situation. It was the Allies' failure to realise the tempo of mechanised operations, rather than a deficiency in the means, that proved the decisive factor.

Anyone who really understood this new *tempo* could easily have foiled the German break-through—for the Allies at the start had six mechanised divisions at hand (with two more available) and seventeen motorised divisions against the Germans' ten mechanised and seven motorised. There had also been ample time beforehand to block the German approach routes with mines, or even by the simple device of felling the trees along the forest-roads through the Ardennes to the Meuse—a proposal that was urged on the French High Command but rejected on the ground of keeping the routes clear for their own cavalry's advance!

It was not the Germans' superior concentration of numbers on this sector that produced the result. That fact is very clear. For both the break-in and the break-through were achieved by the small fraction of mechanised divisions *before* the mass of the German infantry divisions, marching on foot and with horse transport, came into action. Moreover, although mechanisation and motorisation offered a *potential* advantage in rapid switching of force to achieve local superiority of force, that kind of strategic mobility did not play any important part in the 1940 break-through. No such sudden switching of force took place until after the Meuse line had been pierced, and then only by two mechanised divisions—switched from the German right wing to reinforce the seven that had already broken through and were sweeping on to the Channel coast in their exploiting drive.

SUBSEQUENT DEVELOPMENTS IN WORLD WAR II

When the other side began to understand the tempo and conditions of mechanised warfare it soon became evident that no radical change had occurred in the basic trend of land warfare in this century and the last—towards a growing material ascendency of defence over attack, *pari passu*, and thus towards a diminishing ratio of force to space required to hold a front securely.

The first evidence was provided in North Africa, by Rommel's frustration in his attacks on Tobruk in April and May, 1941. Here the Ninth Australian Division, with one extra infantry brigade and two small tank regiments—a total of 24,000 fighting troops—held a poorly fortified perimeter of thirty miles (i.e. only 800 men to the mile). Yet it succeeded in repelling an attacking force of two German divisions (both mechanised) and three Italian divisions (one mechanised).

In the attacks launched by the British and Axis forces in turn during the next twelve months of the North African campaign, there was always an open desert flank for

105

out-flanking manoeuvre, and in that way only was success achieved—while several times reversed by counterstroke.

But a very clear test of defence against attack, without a wide open flank, was provided by the Battle of Alam Halfa at the end of August 1942, and the 2nd Battle of Alamein in October.

In the first case, Rommel's attack suffered a severe repulse from Montgomery's defence, with a force of similar strength.

In the second case, Rommel defended a length of nearly forty miles with a fighting strength of 27,000 Germans and 50,000 Italians—a ratio of 2,000 to a mile of front (though the 50,000 poorly equipped and dispirited Italians counted in reality much less than the 27,000 Germans). In terms of normal-scale divisions, the ratio was equivalent to one division for every eight miles of front (and for those in the line, a ratio of one to every sixteen miles).

Montgomery, now greatly reinforced, attacked this thin (but well-mined) front with a superiority of 8 to 1 in fighting troops over the Germans—3 to 1 over Germans and Italians together—and 6 to 1 in effective tanks. Yet, even with this immense superiority, the attack only succeeded after thirteen days' struggle, and by sheer attrition—losing three times as many tanks as the defender in the process of wearing down the defender's tank strength to vanishing point.

In the Normandy campaign, analysis shows that Allied attacks hardly ever succeeded unless the attacking troops had a superiority of more than 5 to 1 in fighting strength— even though they were greatly helped by complete domination of the air (which at least doubles the value of ground forces, and in some staff calculations has been reckoned as trebling it). In some cases, attacks failed with odds of nearly 10 to 1 in their favour—as in " Operation Bluecoat ", the ably planned break-out attempt by the British Second Army near Caumont on July 30, 1944, to coincide with the

American break-out thrust at Avranches. The ten-mile sector attacked was held by one depleted German division. Yet the massive blow failed to overcome the thin defence except on the Western part of the sector, and even there it was checked on the third day when meagre tank reinforcements at last began to arrive on the German side.

During much of this time the defender's ratio of force to hold the eighty-mile stretch of the Normandy front was only equivalent to one normal-scale division to eight miles on the average. Once the break-out was eventually achieved, after eight weeks' struggle, the German reserves were so scanty, and the space for outflanking manoeuvre so wide, that the Allied armies were able to advance almost unhindered, especially on the right or inland wing. Their progress was all the easier because the bulk of the German divisions were not even motorised—unlike the Allied divisions. But when the approaches to the Rhineland were reached, the Allies were brought to a halt, and kept at bay, by the motley forces that the German Command scraped up. These improvised forces succeeded in holding frontages wider than had ever been thought practicable before. Thus the war was prolonged, unexpectedly, for a further eight months.

On the Eastern Front the Russian armies, in their turn, had been disrupted by the deep and swift thrusts of the panzer forces in the summer of 1941. But before the year ended, they were learning how to check these thrusts, and in 1942 developed the appropriate counter-technique.

But when the Russians' renewed and increasing reserves enabled them to change over to the offensive, they were faced by opponents who knew the technique. Even though the Russians benefited from the exceptionally wide space of the Eastern Front, the defence repelled attacks delivered with a superiority of 7 to 1, or even more. Moreover, the German panzer divisions, by virtue of their mechanised mobility, often succeeded in covering and defending frontages up to twenty miles, against very heavy odds.

Analysis of the basic data of the campaigns in World War II points to conclusions very different from the surface appearance of events. They have an important bearing on the present defence problem of NATO, in face of Russia's great superiority of numbers.

It is, of course, obvious that any numerical calculation of strength—in divisions or men—is subject to a variety of other important factors—particularly equipment, terrain, area, communications, training, tactical methods, leadership, *and* morale. These factors are far more variable, and thus more difficult to calculate, than numbers or length of front.

The obvious difficulty presented by such " variables " was always brought up by the General Staff as an insuperable objection whenever the idea of operational research, based on the method of quantitative analysis, was urged in the years before World War II. Yet once it was accepted, and belatedly started, its value came to be appreciated amply— first by the Air Staff, then by the Naval Staff, and eventually by the General Staff. The practical benefit of quantitative analysis of the quantitative factors became very clear, and was not impaired by the " variables " in any such degree as had been imagined.

It is worth bearing in mind this experience when considering the possibilities of a " force to space ratio " analysis. Everyone who has to make plans in war or exercises, from the Supreme Command down to the platoon leader, actually works on a " force to space " calculation—but it is a rough rule-of-thumb calculation, in which the *norm* is apt to be a product of custom and habit. It is desirable to replace that hazy proceeding by a norm derived from scientifically analysed data—a better basis on which to make suitable allowance for, and adjustment to, the variables.

If such a basis had been worked out before the last war, it would have been a check on such a fatal miscalculation as was made in the distribution of the Allied forces on the Western Front in 1940 and apportioning the fraction that covered the Allied centre on the Meuse.

By the middle of the war the need for a norm as a basis of calculation came to be recognised, and a broad guidance on force ratios was formulated in the British official manual on *Umpiring*. But it needs to be re-examined, clarified, and more fully defined.

11

AMPHIBIOUS FLEXIBILITY AND FORCES

THE Pacific campaign in World War II has long been recognised as a superb demonstration of the strategic value of amphibious flexibility. It is very clear that without the distracting and the by-passing power it conferred—the ability to vary the thrust-point while keeping the opponent on the stretch—the penetration of Japan's successive outlying defence-line would have been a far slower and more costly process.

In contrast, the war in Europe is regarded as mainly a continental land struggle, determined by the direct action of the armies and air forces, in which sea power merely played a subsidiary role as the means of conveying troops and supplies to feed the fight. Moreover, in the familiar picture of the war, such part as sea power played appears to be of relatively little importance as an influence on the Eastern Front —the only fighting front in Europe until late in 1943, and the one where the largest part of the German Army continued to be engaged until the end of the war.

But analysis of the distribution of Germany's strength at successive stages of the war leads to very different conclusions, and changes the picture. From such analysis it becomes evident that the amphibious flexibility provided by sea power, which the Western allies possessed, exerted a much greater influence than appears on the surface of events.

In May 1940 the Germans massed 65 per cent. of their strength in the armies deployed to invade France and the

Low Countries, leaving only 5 per cent. to guard their rear against the Russian armies that had advanced into and occupied the eastern half of Poland. That immensely disproportionate distribution was not due to unreserved trust in the Russians' peaceful intentions, but to the temporary insurance provided by their own large strategic reserve (OKH Reserve) amounting to 30 per cent. of their total strength in divisions. For, although it was handily placed to back up the offensive in the West, part of it could have been quickly switched eastward to Poland if the Russians had made any threatening move on that front. The distance between the two fronts was not large. Moreover, when it became quite clear that no Russian move in Poland was developing, the Germans were emboldened to use the whole of this reserve to support their advance into the West, so that 95 per cent. of their strength was eventually committed there.

A very significant difference was seen in the Germans' deployment, and proportionate concentration, for the invasion of Russia in 1941. Here, only 60 per cent. (120 divisions) of their strength was launched in the offensive, and only 13 per cent. (twenty-six divisions) was in strategic reserve—to reinforce the attacking armies. For 27 per cent. of the German strength (fifty-three divisions) was standing guard in the sea-girdled and sea-menaced areas of western, north-western and south-eastern Europe—an 8,000 mile stretch of coastline.

That large subtraction from the concentration against Russia was of great detriment to Germany's chances of victory and of great help to Russia's chances of withstanding attack. It became of increasingly vital importance once Russia succeeded in surviving the first onslaught.

Such a conclusion is not a claim for the *actual* effect of what Britain, the only survivor of the original Western alliance, did to draw German strength away from the

Russian front. Her efforts were small, and their effect slighter than has been claimed by Churchill, Alanbrooke and other British military chiefs, or their spokesmen. These overclaims have obscured, or at least blurred, the basic fact—and basic lesson. For the vital subtraction was really due to the widespread threat, and consequent distraction, inherent in sea power and its essential complement, amphibious flexibility of striking power against any sea-coast stretches. It was the potential threat that had the actual effect.

Further significant points, and lessons, emerge in closer examination of the 1941 situation, at the time that the Germans embarked on the invasion of Russia. In the first place the detailed distribution of the subtracted strength is worth study and emphasis.

In France and the Low Countries were stationed thirty-eight divisions—19 per cent. of the Germans' total field army. In Norway and Denmark there were eight divisions—a further 4 per cent. of the total. In neither of these areas was the subtraction due to any imminent counter-invasion that the British looked likely to make, or were capable of making in the period of gradual recuperation from the 1940 disaster in France, when they had lost most of their equipment although they had managed to extricate most of their troops. But the largeness of the subtraction to guard these areas cannot, alternatively, be ascribed simply to the fact that they consisted of countries recently conquered and occupied by the Germans, which had to be held down. For at this time the resistance movements in these countries were causing no serious trouble, and were not as formidable as in Poland, where the Germans had, nevertheless, dared to reduce their forces much more, when striking westward in 1940, despite having simultaneously to hold down the Poles and keep on guard against the Russians.

Thus it is difficult to see any factor that can be credited

112

with major effect on the subtraction, except the mental impression, on Continental minds, of the inherent threat and instinctive stretch produced by seapower *plus* amphibious flexibility. That inference is reinforced by the fact that of the eight divisions posted in the Scandinavian area, only one was in Denmark, while seven were in Norway—which presented a far longer and more exposed coastline to seaborne countermoves. It is the *potential* effectiveness of the threat, and disturbance, that best explains the seven-fold difference in the protective strength allocated by the Germans to Norway as compared with Denmark—where a British landing would have been a closer menace to Germany itself, but was much more difficult to gain and maintain, as the Germans realised.

In the Mediterranean theatre the Germans left nine divisions at the time they invaded Russia. Seven of these were in the Balkans, which Hitler had been impelled to invade, before tackling Russia, by his fear of a British sea-borne threat to the flank of his advance into Russia and to the Rumanian oilfields on which his forces depended for fuel. Although he had expelled the British from Greece he continued to fear a renewal of the threat, and his Balkan detachment would have been larger still but for the fact that his Italian allies took a big share in garrisoning that area.

The other two German divisions in the Mediterranean theatre formed the panzer group that had recently been dispatched overseas, under Rommel's command, to support the Italian army in North Africa after its shattering defeat by the British. That small detachment proved a profitable strategic investment, in contrast to the much larger ones elsewhere. For it not only saved the Italians from complete collapse and preserved the Axis position in North Africa for a further two years, but developed a threat to the British hold on Egypt and the Suez Canal which drew thither more than twenty divisions from Britain's reserves—nearly half her operational strength. It was by far the most effective distraction that Germany produced in the war, and one of the most striking examples in history of what can be achieved in that way by an oversea expedition. Even so, it was far from equalling the overall balance of distraction produced, to the Germans' disadvantage, merely by the threat of amphibious flexibility—that potential which had been Britain's greatest asset in all her wars, and which was now greatly augmented by American reinforcement.

Seapower made possible the combined American and British landings on the coast of French North Africa, in November 1942, and then trapped the German and Italian forces in Tunisia, ensuring that the whole of them were " put in the bag "—in May 1943. That result cleared the way for the Allies' re-entry into Europe, by eliminating the bulk of the forces which would otherwise have faced the Allies in Sicily—and might easily have blocked their capture of that stepping stone. The successful landing in Sicily, two months later, produced the downfall of Mussolini and the quickly following surrender of Italy.

The Allies' follow-up on the mainland of Italy, and her breakaway from alliance with Germany, immediately drew eighteen German divisions into Italy in an effort to check the Allies' invasion—made with fifteen divisions—while the German forces in the Balkans were also doubled, being brought up to fifteen divisions there, as a protective measure. That was a good balance of distraction in the Allies' favour.

But in Italy itself the balance tilted the opposite way when the Allied armies suffered repeated and prolonged checks in their effort to advance up the narrow peninsula. To revive the advance, in 1944, the Allies poured thirty divisions into Italy against the Germans' twenty-two which were, on the average, barely two-thirds the strength of Allied divisions. Although that swelling reinforcement now, at last, succeeded in levering the Germans out of Rome, and driving them back to the Gothic Line in the mountain belt north of Florence—where they held on until the following year—the invasion of Italy had ceased to pay a good strategic dividend in propor- to the resources invested in it.

Nevertheless, the Allies' amphibious power had, in other respects, achieved an increasing strategic effect on the situa- tion as a whole, to Germany's detriment and Russia's bene- fit. For at the beginning of June 1944, before any other Allied landing had taken place, only 55 per cent. (165 divi- sions) of the German Army* remained on the Eastern Front, to meet the increasing pressure of the Russians' tidal ad- vance, while nearly 45 per cent. (133 divisions) had been drawn westward or southward to guard against the threat of Anglo-American seaborne invasion.

It is also very significant that, of the total, barely 10 per cent. (thirty-two divisions) was posted in the northern part of France (north of the Loire) to meet the impending cross- Channel attack. Moreover, only 6 per cent. (eighteen divi- sions) was employed with the two armies that held the front in central Italy against the Allied offensive there.

In contrast, eighteen divisions were posted in Norway and Denmark; nine in the Low Countries; eight in the south- west of France covering the Biscay coast; ten in the south- east of France covering the Mediterranean coast; ten cover- ing the Mediterranean and Adriatic coasts of Northern Italy; and a further twenty-eight in the south-east of Europe, another area which presented a long coastline to potential seaborne invasion. This total of eighty-three divisions was a subtraction of German strength produced mainly by the looming shadow of possible seaborne attack by the Western allies—for partisan activity was formidable only in

---

* The total number of divisions had been increased from 200 in 1941 to approximately 300 by 1944, but divisional strengths were reduced.

115

Yugoslavia. Such a vast distraction, nearly 30 per cent. of Germany's total resources, was tremendous testimony to the effect of amphibious flexibility.

It is worth note, however, that when the Allies actually landed, their distraction effect did not increase proportionately to the effort made, and in some cases began to diminish soon after the landing. That diminishing return was most marked in the Italian campaign—where, after the opening phase, the Allies were employing a much larger force than that opposing their advance. The unfavourable turn was due partly to the narrowness of the Italian peninsula. The basic lesson is that *offensive* distraction is more effective *when* it carries a wide strategic threat, and *where* there is ample room for its development by attack to be expanded easily and quickly into a widening tactical threat.

But the comparatively poor distraction effect of the Italian campaign, after the landing, was also due to diminishing amphibious power in the Mediterranean theatre. Italy would have been a more suitable site for attack if there had been ample assault shipping, and for a long enough time. But when the decision was made to land there, the planners had already committed themselves to an undertaking that most of the assault shipping which was available should be moved back to harbours in Britain in readiness for the cross-Channel attack. The key importance of adequate amphibious means is another basic lesson of modern warfare.

" Adequate amphibious means " are not only a matter of ships. Skilled personnel are of no less importance, and they need to be available in adequate numbers if landing operations are to be executed smoothly and exploited quickly. The required skill is the fruit of long training in amphibious techniques, and of constant practice in combination of the various elements in such a force.

In studying the African, Sicilian, Salerno and Anzio

116

landings, it becomes evident that many hitches and delays occurred from lack of knowledge and experience in dealing with amphibious problems, and from differences of view between the Army and the Navy commanders and staffs respectively. At Salerno, the first time when tough opposition was met, a costly check was suffered and a crisis developed —so grave that General Mark Clark described it, even in cool retrospect, as " a near disaster ". Only by a narrow margin did the landing force hold off the German counter-attack and avoid being driven back into the sea. Yet the counter-attack did not come until five days after the landing, and was even then delivered by a force much smaller than the Allies had by then placed ashore. At Anzio, four months later, a great opportunity was lost of unhinging the German front by this landing in its rear, near Rome—and then another crisis developed. Yet the Germans were so weak in the area, and so strained in general, that thirteen days passed before the counter-attack was delivered. Such lengthy time lapses offered the Allies ample opportunity to establish and exploit their lodgement, and their failure to profit from the long respite emphasises the inefficiency of these landing operations—in execution as contrasted with conception.

In searching for the explanation, and in comparing the execution with the better performances among Pacific landing operations, a clue can be found in a significant factor there—which was missing in the Mediterranean, and in the European theatre as a whole. For in this theatre there was no specialised amphibious force such as the U.S. Marine Corps divisions provided in the Pacific. A spearhead of such divisions might well have made a striking difference to the rapidity and effectiveness of the landing operations in the European theatre.

That deduction is strengthened in the course of studying British landing operations—not only those in World War II, but throughout the past three hundred years. During these centuries, Britain has, by force of circumstances, particularly her geographical situation, been the most distinctively amphibious of all the powers. Until very recently, the last generation, her Navy was supreme among the fleets of the world, and by it she maintained a world-wide empire—despite the smallness of her island home base. Yet, for all her success at sea, and in expanding overseas, her performance in amphibious warfare did not match her experience of it. Her expeditionary forces more often failed than succeeded in gaining their objectives when they met any serious opposition.

During the hundred years prior to the French Revolution, Britain was repeatedly at war with France—which, under the Bourbons, was not only threatening to dominate the continent of Europe, but also the world overseas. In these struggles, Britain relied on seapower to counterbalance French landpower, and exploited her advantage at sea to achieve compensating gains that could provide bargaining counters in peace negotiations. An examination of the record shows, however, that out of seventeen amphibious expeditions which Britain launched during these hundred years against France and her colonies, only seven attained their objectives. In the twenty years' struggle against Revolutionary and Napoleonic France that followed, only four out of twelve were successful. The most common cause of failure was mutual misunderstanding, of the other Service's problems, between the general in charge of the expeditionary force and the admiral in charge of the escorting fleet, and between their respective subordinates. All too often, the attack miscarried or evaporated in wrangling between the co-operating services—who, through incompatibility of views and loyalties, were apt to become the enemy's best allies.

The record of British amphibious operations was even more disappointing in the next great war, a century later—the First World War. At this time the leaders of the British Army had become so continentally-minded that their governing idea was simply to provide a direct reinforcement to France—the traditional enemy who had now become Britain's ally—by shipping the bulk of the Army across the Channel to fight alongside the French Army. They frowned on the arguments, voiced by Winston Churchill, Admiral " Jacky " Fisher, and Maurice Hankey (the Marine officer who became Secretary of the Committee of Imperial Defence and the War Cabinet) for continuing to follow the historic principles of British strategy—a strategic tradition which had now, in soldiers' eyes, become a heresy. Thus few amphibious operations were attempted, compared with the number in earlier wars; and they did not fulfil expectations, owing, largely, to the continuance of mutual misunderstanding and difference of view between the Services.

The attempt, in October 1914, to save Antwerp from the Germans became a disjointed fiasco. Early in November a seaborne expeditionary force, sent to capture German East Africa, landed at Tanga but was driven to re-embark three days later. After that repulse it was decided to substitute an overland advance, but this took four years to achieve its purpose. Germany's other colonies in Africa were also conquered by overland expeditions, of varying duration, and only her undefended Pacific islands were captured by seaborne moves.

In 1915 the one important amphibious operation of the war was launched—to open the Dardanelles by capturing the Gallipoli peninsula, which commands the gateway to these straits, and knock out Germany's Turkish ally. Amphibious flexibility, and its distracting effect, helped the British to take the Turks off balance both in the original April landing and

119

again in the fresh August landing further up the peninsula. But on each occasion opportunity was forfeited on landing, and a costly stalemate ensued, so at the end of the year the expeditionary force was evacuated.

Even though it failed, the Gallipoli expedition had, by its threat, upset the whole war plan of the Germans for 1915. What success would have meant to the Triple Entente (Britain, France and Russia) is shown by the testimony of General von Falkenhayn, then the directing head of the Germanic alliance: " If the straits between the Mediterranean and the Black Sea were not permanently closed to Entente traffic, all (our) hopes of a successful issue of the war would be seriously diminished. Russia would have been freed from her strategic isolation which . . . offered a surer guarantee than any military success . . . that the forces of this Titan would eventually and automatically be crippled ". That eventual crippling, by 1917, resulted from the way that, in 1915, a farsighted amphibious conception was wrecked by a chain of errors in execution. The consequences were far-reaching, for the crippling of Russia's forces led to the Revolution there and the establishment of the Communist régime.

More immediately, the dismal ending of the Gallipoli expedition caused the British to abandon the idea of renewing their amphibious strategy, and committed them more fully to the grinding and long-drawn attrition campaign on the deeply entrenched Western Front that left both Britain and France exhausted by the time that the war was ended. The only bright amphibious flash in these years was the raid on the Germans' advanced naval base at Zeebrugge in 1918 —on St. George's Day—which was carried out purely by the Navy, with assault companies of Marines.

Between then and the Second World War, the introduction of some measures of joint staff training raised hopes that amphibious operations would be better conducted if war came again. But in 1940 the seaborne moves to counter the German invasion of Norway were as badly bungled as almost any of those in the past. The next important amphibious thrust, that against Dieppe in 1942, was also a depressing fiasco. Subsequent amphibious operations, carried out in conjunction with American forces, have already been examined and discussed.

It is strange, and puzzling, that Britain's performance in amphibious operations during the course of these three centuries should have been so poor in comparison with the achievement of her Navy on the seas, and also of her Army in many of the battles it fought on foreign soil, when operating on its own—out of reach of naval support. The clue to the puzzle can be found in a missing factor, and instrument. For although Britain formed a force of marines as far back as 1664—originally named the " Admiral's regiment "—and although its great value was soon proved, it has always been confined to a very limited scale and scope. It has never been developed, like the U.S. Marine Corps, into a strong amphibious fighting force embodying all the different arms and elements required for effective attacking power, and capable of carrying out a large-scale landing operation. An explanation of Britain's oft-repeated failure in such operations can be seen in her neglect to develop the Royal Marines in this way, and for this purpose. Moreover, no other explanation becomes apparent in studying the record.

The official neglect, or reluctance, to develop them is the more strange because their value was so amply acknowledged by famous expeditionary commanders. Indeed, Admiral Vernon was so impressed that in 1739 he urged " the necessity of converting most of our marching regiments into marines ". In 1802 they were made a royal corps on the recommendation of that great commander and strategist,

121

Lord St. Vincent, who declared: " There never was an appeal made to them for honour, courage or loyalty, that they did not more than realise my highest expectations. If ever real danger should come to England, the marines will be found the country's sheet-anchor." In default of their expansion on an adequate scale, he urged that England's next best policy, as an amphibious power, would be to make every infantry regiment serve afloat as marines, in rotation, as part of their duty. In 1804, on Nelson's recommendation, a corps of artillery was added to the Royal Marines for duty both in ships and ashore. Their performance in the shore role was so good that Napier, the soldier historian of the Peninsular War, frankly acknowledged that " Never in my life have I seen soldiers like the Royal Marine Artillery ". But sixteen years after the war, when its lessons were fading, the Royal Marine Artillery was abolished as a measure of economy—although subsequently revived after further reflection on experience.

Why is it that in Britain, the country most dependent on seapower, the marines have never been developed in adequate scale and scope, as they have been in America? The basic hindrance has been that opposing vested interests, which are strong everywhere, are reinforced by the distrust of specialisation that is a British characteristic. The Services, and particularly the Army, have always been inclined to resist specialist claims and specialised forces.

If compelled by necessity to accept these, the Army has sought to discard them as soon as possible—and usually too soon. It maintains its faith in the " general purpose " concept—the idea and ideal that *every* man should be capable of fitting *any* job, and be a " jack of all trades ". Linked with such disregard of differing aptitudes has been an ingrained distrust of those who mastered any special technique—often prompted by an underlying fear that recognition of its importance would disqualify for promotion those who had not

122

acquired it. This very common attitude is reinforced by the repugnance which armies have constantly shown towards new methods and new instruments. Even when something new could no longer be resisted, its further development has too often been handed over to a general " handyman " who would not be likely to make the most of its potentialities.

The most significant development of the nineteenth century was the introduction of light infantry—nimble sharpshooters who skirmished ahead of the line, using cover and individual aimed fire, to harass the close-packed ranks of the enemy's line or massive columns, and thus pave their way for the advance of their own. A light company was added to each battalion. Then, profiting from bitter experience in the American backwoods, some of the more progressive British officers secured the formation of regiments composed entirely of light infantry. Nursed by Sir John Moore, they were formed into an *élite* force—the famous Light Division of the Peninsular War, which surpassed all other infantry in its combined exploitation of mobility and firepower. But during the long peace that followed, the force was broken up and the regiments were brought back into conformity of role and tactics with the ordinary infantry—retaining only their distinctive title, tradition, a more flexible system of drill, and a faster pace.

Towards the end of the nineteenth century, the invention of the machine-gun foreshadowed another radical change in tactics, but when it was at last adopted in the British Army, it was parcelled out among the infantry, two to a battalion. These little special packets did not fit into the battalion pattern, and on exercises the only orders that the machine-gun officer was apt to get were: " Take the damned things away and hide 'em." They were not effectively used until a Machine Gun Corps was formed late in 1915, after more than a year of war. And when the war ended the Corps was disbanded.

The most revolutionary invention in that war was the tank. But the personnel of this new arm were at first organised only as a branch of the Machine Gun Corps, and even when a Tank Corps was created in 1917 as a recognition of what it had achieved, it was maintained on a temporary basis for a further six years. Only in 1923 did the Army Council, after much hesitation, agree to it being made permanent—as the Royal Tank Corps. But it was kept on a very small scale. Sixteen years later, on the eve of World War II, it was merged with the cavalry, who were belatedly converted from horses and much more numerous, in a common frame entitled the Royal Armoured Corps. The resulting scarcity, and dilution, of expert knowledge and experience in Britain's Armoured Corps goes far to explain why, despite its pioneer achievements, its performance as a whole in World War II compared poorly with the German—which, although not formed until 1933, was treated as an *élite* force from that time on.

From Gideon to Guderian, the value of *élite* forces has been repeatedly demonstrated in warfare. The " 300 " that formed " The *sword* of the Lord, and of Gideon " in defeating the host of Midian were picked, out of ten thousand, by the way they gave evidence of exceptional dash. The Royal Companions (cavalry) and Royal Hypaspists (foot) played a decisive part in Alexander the Great's unbroken run of victories. So did the Guards division in Genghiz Khan's. Cromwell's Ironsides of the New Model, Napoleon's Imperial Guard, Ludendorff's storm troops in the German break-through attacks of 1918, and Guderian's Panzers in 1940, are among the other successive links in the historical chain of evidence that proves the value of having *élite* forces for tasks of key importance.

The British, however, have long shown an obstinate

disfavour for the concept, except in its application to the social sphere. Although the Foot Guards have a very fine military record, they would hardly have survived but for their intimate association with the monarchy. In war, the British have paid heavily for their reluctance to recognise the need and value of special skills—and in no respect have they paid so heavily as in amphibious operations.

The Americans have adjusted their forces far better to changing conditions and new needs, especially in the amphibious sphere. The development of the Marine Corps as a spearhead force in this sphere, embodying all the various elements required for timely effect, has been a striking example. It is a model of how special problems should be tackled by special means.

It was through seapower and its " companion "—the power to carry by sea a force that can be thrown ashore wherever desired or needed—that for centuries Britain helped her friends on the Continent to resist aggression, and averted its domination by any single nation or tyrant. The same coupled power also enabled this small island country of very limited strength to maintain a world-wide network of colonies and protectorates.

In World War II this coupled power, immensely reinforced when the United States came into the war alongside Britain, was basically the decisive factor in liberating Europe from Hitler's tyranny, as well as in liberating the Far East from Japan's. For airpower then had not the range to exert its effect until bases were gained within close enough reach of the enemy for it to operate effectively, while Russia's land-power was not enough by itself to overthrow him.

After the war, the older kinds of military power were for a time overshadowed—and in the public's eye eclipsed—by the development of nuclear power, conveyed by air. But nuclear power was too drastic and dangerous for use except as a last resort, even while it remained a monopoly, and thus in many respects unsuitable as a counter to insidious or limited forms of aggression. So seapower and its amphibious companion continued to be the operative means for curbing aggression against any of the free countries on the Eurasian land mass. Their prospects of protection have depended more on being within supporting reach from the sea than on the shadowy, and boomerang, threat of a nuclear retort.

Now that Russia has produced nuclear weapons in large quantity to match America's, and taken the lead with inter-Continental missiles, a nuclear stalemate has developed. In these circumstances, local and limited aggression becomes more likely, while amphibious forces become more necessary, both as a deterrent and as a counter to it—a counter which can be used without being suicidal, and a deterrent which is therefore credible.

On a superficial view, airborne forces may appear to be a better counter, as being quicker to arrive. But their speed of strategic movement, and effect on arrival, are subject to many limitations.

Many of the spots where an emergency may arise are far distant, and cannot be reached by air without flying over foreign territory or making a long circuit to avoid it. Most of the Asiatic and African countries are acutely sensitive to any infringement of their recently acquired independence, resentful of Western interference in those regions, and insistent on preserving neutrality, or apt to side with the opponents of the West. A circuitous air approach, even where possible, increases the need for intermediate bases, where aircraft can be refuelled and serviced, while their establishment and maintenance are subject to similar political difficulties.

Strategic movement by air is so *liable* to be blocked or impeded by countries in its path that it is becoming strategically *unreliable* as a way of meeting the world-wide problems of the Atlantic Alliance—which, more truly should be called the Oceanic Alliance.

Moreover, on arrival, an airborne force needs airfields for its disembarkation and logistic support. Adequate ones for large aircraft and a large force do not exist in many areas, and even when they do they may be in hostile hands. If well defended, an attempt to capture them by parachute drop can easily turn into disaster, while a ground approach may be checked through lack of tactical mobility and of weapon-power sufficient to overcome strong resistance. For an airborne force is narrowly limited in the vehicles, heavy weapons, and ammunition it can carry. If it is held up and has to wait for these requirements to arrive by sea, it loses its main advantage—rapidity of intervention. Another of its drawbacks is its vulnerability to interception while in transit. On top of all comes the high cost of strategic air movement—for one division, twenty times what it costs by sea for a medium-range move of about 2,000 miles, and forty times for long-range moves of about 8,000 miles.

In tackling emergencies two hands are better than one—and essential when one is unreliable. While it is desirable to have an airborne force, which enables quicker intervention where its use is possible, it is essential to have a marine force —and better that this should be the bigger of the two. For the bigger it is the more possible becomes a strategic deployment wide enough and strong enough to ensure early and effective intervention wherever there is a blaze, and before it spreads. An amphibious force of modern type, operating from the sea and equipped with helicopters, is free from dependence on airfields, beaches, ports, land-bases—with all their logistical and political complications. The use of an airborne force, or of any land-based force, is a more irrevocable step, since its commitment is more definite and its withdrawal more difficult. A self-contained and sea-based amphibious force, of which the U.S. Marine Corps is the prototype, is the best kind of fire-extinguisher—because of its flexibility, reliability, logistic simplicity, and relative economy.

Finally, it may be useful to summarise the principal conclusions that emerge from an extensive study of war history, past and contemporary, and in particular of the part that sea-based powers have played—

> Amphibious flexibility is the greatest strategic asset that a sea-based power possesses. It creates a distraction to a continental enemy's concentration that is most advantageously disproportionate to the resources employed.
>
> The distracting effect is apt to diminish, however, after a landing takes place unless this is made in an area spacious enough for its expansion into a widening threat, and unless its exploitation is rapid—particularly in the opening phase. The best way to ensure such initial rapidity lies in the use of a specialised amphibious force—and the need for it is now greater than ever before. Although Britain has, by force of geographical circumstances, been more amphibious in action than any other power, her performance has been much poorer than her experience. That deficiency is due to her failure to develop her marines into a special " lock-opening " force of adequate scale. The United States has been wiser in this important respect.
>
> The value of such a force is endorsed by the sum of experience through the ages about the value of *élite* forces in general. Their key importance as lock-openers has been repeatedly proved in the history of warfare, and more than ever in recent times.
>
> No fresh problem in war has been effectively tackled if treated in a " general purpose " way, and entrusted to a Service or arm primarily concerned with other and more

128

familiar problems that habitually come within its sphere. The unhappy history of armoured forces, particularly in Britain and France, is a recent example—and lesson. Amphibious warfare is one of the basic problems that call for specialised treatment.

These conclusions lead on to a further reflection. It has come to be recognised that the old distinction between land and sea operations is no longer suitable. But the recent three-fold division into land, sea, and air operations fits no better and is already out of date. While operational problems are different, their differences cannot be solved on three separate lines. Problems need to be tackled in a more integrated way, blending the functions of the three Services.

The U.S. Marine Corps is a three-in-one Service in embryo. It has gained so much experience in combining land, sea and air action that it forms a nucleus and a pattern for further development. Logically it should be the basis for further progress in integration. Any reduction of its scale and function would be a retrograde step. For it is the most important advance in military organisation since the " divisional system "—the division of an army into self-contained fractions, embodying all arms and capable of fighting independently—was introduced near the end of the eighteenth century, and became the key instrument of Napoleon's operations.

PART THREE

THE NATO SHIELD

12

CAN NATO PROTECT US TODAY?

NATO was born on April 4, 1949, when the North Atlantic Treaty was signed in Washington by the representatives of twelve countries. Eight of these starters were on the European mainland—France, Belgium, the Netherlands, Luxemburg, Italy, Portugal, Denmark and Norway. The others were Britain, Iceland, Canada and the United States. Three more countries have joined this collective defence " club " since then—Greece and Turkey in 1952 ; Federal Germany in 1955.

NATO was the offspring of the Berlin crisis—the Soviet blockade of West Berlin, maintained for eleven months, and foiled only by the large-scale and sustained Allied air lift that was organised to meet the emergency. The Korean crisis of 1950 produced a further spur, and the creation of a Supreme Headquarters for the Allied Powers in Europe— SHAPE for short. SHAPE officially came into existence one minute after midnight on April 2, 1951—a birth that would seem to have been timed to avoid the proverbial risks of April Fools' Day.

The North Atlantic Treaty specified in Article 12 that after it had been in force for ten years it should be reviewed, at the request of any member-state in " regard to the factors then affecting peace and security ". Article 13, however, laid down that only after twenty years could any member-state withdraw from the Treaty, after giving a year's notice.

It is certainly desirable that there should be a review of the

133

Treaty, its value and present effectiveness, in the light of over ten years' experience and of present conditions. A new Berlin crisis may loom up any time, and would be the more serious since Kruschev has already given warning that no air lift will this time be tolerated, as a loophole, if the road and rail routes to West Berlin are blocked. He has the means of applying the screw very hard unless he obtains a settlement of the whole German situation, and problem, satisfactory to Russia.

A review of NATO must start with the question of its value in comparison to cost up to the present time. Militarily, the product has been very poor—appallingly small for the outlay. The creation of NATO can only be justified on less tangible and testable grounds. Since 1949 the member-countries have spent an immensely increased amount of money on defence. For the countries in Western Europe alone it has risen to the sterling equivalent of £4,000 million a year—of which Britain has been contributing more than £1,500 million.

Despite this vast expenditure, the NATO " shield force " covering the heart of Europe has fallen far short of the minimum defensive strength that was considered essential when SHAPE plans were framed. It has never provided a hopeful chance of effective and prolonged defence against a major attack by the Russian forces which face it.

The spur to the creation of NATO, during the Berlin crisis of 1948-9, was a realisation that if the Russians were to advance westward they could swamp the Western Powers' ground defences, and sweep through to the Channel coast without any check. For they had about thirty divisions poised in occupied territory behind the Iron Curtain, and over 100 more available to draw upon in European Russia, supported by some 6,000 aircraft—whereas the Western Powers, since demobilising, had in all only about fourteen divisions on the Continent, and these were far from a state of readiness for action, while they had less than 1,000 aircraft.

Yet now, after more than ten years of building-up NATO, there is still no adequate defence against any major attack on the main front in Central Europe.

The Russians maintain almost as many active divisions as they did before—twenty in East Germany, eight in other satellite countries, and about 100 in European Russia. Moreover, all the divisions in the forward areas, and many of those behind, have been entirely re-equipped with post-war types of weapon, and have had their mobility multiplied by being provided with ample mechanised transport.

By contrast, the NATO forces on the central front have been built up to a strength of barely twenty divisions and that total includes the seven West German divisions that have now been formed. Of this meagre total, only the five American divisions are at full strength and immediately ready for action. The British, now reduced to the equivalent of three, are the next best in strength and readiness. But the Belgian (2) and Netherlands (1) divisions suffer from larger deficiencies and would be subject to more delay in an emergency. The worst deficiency is on the part of the French—who originally undertook to contribute twenty divisions, half of them in a state of immediate readiness, but now have only two on the spot, incomplete and unready. That is largely, although not wholly, due to the drain of the Colonial war in Algeria.

In sum, the military effort of the NATO countries has been a very bad lapse from the original SHAPE plan, approved at the 1952 NATO conference in Lisbon, of building up a ground force of ninety divisions, of which nearly sixty were earmarked to defend the central front.

The great deficiency in number of divisions is multiplied by many defects of organisation. The existing divisions vary in size, mobility, equipment and weapon-power. The time required for mobilisation in the different national armies varies from three to forty-five days. The difference in types of weapon, types of vehicles, and supply systems are a great handicap to strategic flexibility—making it difficult to move divisions from one sector to another. It is hard to imagine such a mixed force maintaining a prolonged resistance, if it were also heavily outnumbered.

NATO's southern flank in Italy is better guarded, as there are here some fifteen divisions to hold a relatively short front, which is covered by mountains. Italy is the only Continental member-country of NATO that has provided its agreed quota under the original plan. But its security is dependent on the strength and firmness of the central front.

As for NATO'S northern flank, in Norway and Denmark, this is much weaker still. There is virtually no defence here against a strong surprise attack. That is the more serious since this flank covers the exits to the Atlantic available for Russia's large submarine forces. The Baltic exit through the Kattegat is of key importance in preventing their emergence onto the seaborne traffic routes of the West, and Britain's in particular.

The basic truth of the situation is that throughout all these years Free Europe's safety has really depended on the *deterrent* effect of the U.S. strategic air force—its power to answer any Russian aggression on the ground by retaliating with nuclear bombs against the Russians' homeland. The huge outlay on the NATO ground forces and tactical air force has counted for little, if anything, as a defence or as a contribution to the deterrent. The most that can be claimed for it is that the feeling of doing something towards their own protection may have helped to maintain the morale of the European peoples, in face of Soviet menace—even though this feeling rested on an illusion, as regards the protective value of their own military shield.

136

Can NATO Protect us Today?

But now a new and much bigger question has arisen—whether the NATO countries can rely any longer on the protection hitherto provided by the deterrent power of the U.S. strategic air force. That vital question was blazoned in the sky by the successful launching of the Sputnik in October 1957, and brought out more emphatically by the striking performance of the Lunik, the moon-rocket, that was launched in January 1959.

These Russian achievements in the new science of rocketry have shattered the prime premise on which Western defence policy has proceeded, in building up its strategic organisation —the complacent assumption that America has, and will continue to have, a strong superiority to Russia in nuclear weapons and the ability to deliver them to their targets. A comfortable assurance has been expressed on this score year after year, and has even been reiterated frequently during the past twelve months.

Now that Russia has taken the lead in the rocket field, as a counterbalance to America's strategic air force, the very large and long-existing numerical superiority of Russia and her allies in ground forces becomes much more formidable. The combination is likely to strengthen her confidence, and theirs, in their ability to develop pressure on the West with impunity. That in itself tends to make local incursions, and minor wars, more likely. It may even foster a belief in the possibility of conducting a larger-scale invasion without such risk as hitherto of bringing on nuclear war.

In the past, American military spokesmen have often declared that their forces would retort with nuclear weapons to any attack on countries or places in the NATO area. More recently the qualifying phrase " major attack " has been used, although still with the implication that even a local frontier incursion would be met with nuclear action if other means did not quickly suffice to stop it, and compel a withdrawal.

137

Moreover, most of the training of the NATO forces during the last five years has been based on the assumption that nuclear weapons will be used, and immediately, against any aggressive move.

Whenever the slightest doubt has been voiced about possible American hesitation, to retort in this way, it has been indignantly contradicted, on every level. Little regard has been paid to the approaching state of nuclear parity-nullity, or stalemate, which has now arrived.

Would an American government venture to launch its nuclear weapons to stop an encroachment upon, or even a strong invasion of, the territory of a small ally abroad— once it realises the likelihood of such a retort precipitating a nuclear counterstroke upon its own now accessible, and very vulnerable, homeland ? Will its small allies abroad continue to believe that their American protector would, if it came to the point, take such a suicidal risk on their behalf ? More important still, will the Russians believe it ? To the coldly calculating men in the Kremlin, such extreme self-sacrifice must look so nonsensical as to be improbable.

Much depends, therefore, on whether the men in the Kremlin take due account of emotional reactions, and pressures, on the other side. History shows that these can make nations disregard all reasoned considerations of self-interest, and even self-preservation. Kruschev and the other conductors of Soviet policy would be wise to remember Hitler's fatal miscalculation in 1939—based on the assumption that the British were too rational to plunge into war, and risk their own destruction, in fulfilment of a hasty promise to Poland. Not only Hitler, but Stalin too, then failed to reckon with the emotional surge that swept Neville Chamberlain's government into war—in the most unfavourable circumstances, and regardless of the disastrous consequences. The best hope for the world now, in the potentially suicidal nuclear age, is that Stalin's successors may take account of that lesson, as well as of the American people's quicker and more intense emotional reactions.

Such a reckoning would form much the strongest check upon a Soviet invasion of NATO territory. But the development of nuclear stalemate makes it of vital importance to strengthen and improve—in efficiency and readiness for action—the NATO ground forces' capacity of checking any local encroachment or pounce that the Russian, or satellite forces, might attempt, emboldened by the new balance of power in the nuclear field resulting from their lead in long-range rockets.

For the primary danger today is of an accidental rather than of a deliberately planned nuclear war. This danger lies in the possibility that some small aggressive move, unless quickly curbed and quenched, might develop unintentionally into nuclear war.

Unfortunately, the problem has been complicated and the danger increased by the expedient of trying to compensate the insufficiency of the shield force by arming it with tactical atomic weapons. That device was adopted with insufficient thought, about its consequences. It has been " sold " to the NATO Governments, and their peoples, with more persuasiveness of salesmanship than logic.

None of the Service chiefs nor the heads of SHAPE have produced any convincing reason for believing that tactical atomic weapons would be able to stop an invasion without recourse to all-out, and therefore suicidal, nuclear war. On the contrary, they have repeatedly in their public utterances shown that they regard it as impracticable to differentiate between the so-called tactical and strategic weapons, and their employment.

It is thus hard to see how the adoption of tactical nuclear-weapons strengthens the *deterrent* to aggression—as the

139

Western military chiefs fondly claim. For if the Russians come to the point of being ready to risk war in face of megaton bombs, either from trust in some new antidote or in nuclear stalemate, it is not likely that they will be deterred by the supplementary check of relatively small kiloton bombs in the tactical field. Indeed, it is more likely that their awareness of SHAPE's conclusion, that differentiation is not practicable, will encourage them to believe that they might safely go a long way in gradual aggression before the NATO statesmen would dare to unleash nuclear weapons of any kind.

Meanwhile SHAPE's conclusion, coupled with its acceptance of the idea that tactical atomic weapons diminish the need for troops, has naturally tended to counteract its own efforts towards building up an adequate shield force. For the dual effect is to dispel any hope of a non-suicidal kind of defence, and deterrent, while fostering a complacent feeling in political quarters that there is neither point nor value in continuing to build up the ground forces.

Now, NATO is faced with the tremendous implications of nuclear stalemate. What will be the principal effects ? The first is to diminish the deterrent to aggression by conventional forces. The second is to increase the potential importance and value of the NATO shield force on the Continent, both as a deterrent and as a defence. The third is to increase the risks of belonging to NATO unless the shield force is made strong enough to repel a Russian attack *without* unleashing nuclear warfare. The development of an inadequate shield force becomes a perilous combination of temptation and provocation. It could become even more fatal in that dual respect than the unfulfillable Anglo-French guarantee to Poland proved in 1939.

For Britain, there are particularly great hazards in commitment to the NATO guarantee of protection to all its extensive and variegated membership. She could all too easily find herself dragged into war to resist some local encroachment or squeeze upon one of the Continental members' territory. So long as the shield force remains inadequate even a small threat of this kind might precipitate general nuclear warfare. In that event, Britain would be the most fatally vulnerable of all countries, because of the industrial density, and dependence on supply through sea-ports, of her small island home-base.

Hence, it is in her own vital interest to make the best possible contribution to the strength of the NATO shield force on the Continent. But it is no less important for her to press that the Continental members should make a proportionate contribution.

At present, the military product of the NATO countries is very poor in proportion to their population. The six countries, other than the United States, which jointly provide the shield force for the central front have a population of 170 millions, but only furnish the equivalent of fifteen divisions for the defence—a mere 190,000 fighting troops. Yet Russia, from a population of 208 millions, produces an estimated 170 divisions—ten times as many in proportion.

What is the cause of the Western countries' failure to create an adequate shield force for their own protection ? It must be lack of will and effort, perilous parsimony, or bad organisation—or a combination of all these deficiencies.

In examination, one finds that the majority of the Continental members of NATO are spending only about 4 per cent. of their gross national product, or income, on their own defence, whereas Britain is spending over 8 per cent. France is now spending the same, but much of it is absorbed by the partisan struggle in Algeria, and her contribution to the direct defence of Europe is dangerously small. If Britain is to continue her commitment to the defence of the Continental countries, with all its growing risks, she has a right to insist that they should spend on their defence at least as much as she is doing.

Another manifest deficiency on their part is the short period of military service. In most of them it is only twelve to eighteen months. That is a great handicap in producing an adequate number of efficient divisions. At least twelve to fifteen months' training is required before soldiers can be capable, in this technical age, of performing their part properly in an operational formation, and it is only after that they really begin to contribute to the effective strength of the shield. A large proportion of the Soviet soldiers have been doing three years' service before going on the reserve, and that is a big factor in producing Russia's very high scale of active divisions.

If the Western countries are not willing to impose such a long period of service on their young men, the alternative is to constitute their first-line forces entirely of long-service professional soldiers—as Britain has decided to do. But her Continental fellow-members of the NATO defence club are reluctant either to increase their length of conscript service to an adequate period or to provide the money for rates of pay required to form an adequate covering force of Regulars.

A further question, no less important, is how far the pitifully small number of operational divisions that NATO has produced is due to bad organisation of the available resources. It is evident that the Russians are getting a much higher proportion of operational divisions out of their man-power, and there is ample reason to suspect that the organisation of the Western armies is inefficient and wasteful. The whole question needs a thorough investigation by impartial experts. If it is to be effective, it must not be entrusted to departmental Service committees which are subject to prevailing vested interests, and habituated to the extravagant establishments of the last war, nor to parliamentary committees and nondescript commissions of inquiry that, through inexperience, can be easily bamboozled.

Given the will, the intelligence, and a thorough re-investigation of the existing organisation, it should be possible to attain the originally planned scale of the NATO shield force. That would provide the West with a non-suicidal form of defence, and a much safer deterrent than it has in its present reliance on the power of nuclear retaliation—which has become nonsensical under the changed conditions produced by Russia's achievement of similar nuclear power, and of an actual lead in missile delivery.

13

CLOUD OVER BERLIN

KRUSCHEV'S recent references to the Berlin problem, although less uncompromising than earlier, show that he remains intent on producing a change in the situation there. That determination is evident in his persistent and reiterated emphasis on Russia's intention to hand over to the East German Government the control of the routes to Berlin, and his declaration that in default of an agreement an Allied air lift to Berlin will not be tolerated, as it was in the crisis of 1948–9.

The Western Governments, Press and people, may have taken these warnings too lightly. They appear to feel that Kruschev is merely indulging in a repetition of the old game of intimidatory bluff, and has no more serious intention of following it up by action than in the past. Are they justified in their comfortable complacency ? Are they right in assuming that if they remain unshaken, and imperturbably continue to mark time, the red lights will always turn to green again ?

Since 1945 the Allied forces in Berlin have been in an extremely awkward situation, tactically untenable—because it is an isolated position that lies deep in Russian-occupied territory. But in the crisis of 1948 the Americans, as the sole possessors of the atomic bomb, had a trump card they could play in any show-down. Now, circumstances have radically changed. Kruschev may feel that they have changed so greatly to Russia's advantage as to make him inclined to carry his pressure further than in the past.

Cloud Over Berlin

The biggest change in circumstances comes from the Russians' startling success in getting ahead of the Americans in the development of accurate long-range missiles. American experts admit that the Russians are now several years ahead of them in this field. The Russians may reckon that their lead is even larger. They may also draw the conclusion that this lead, and their capacity to knock out the great cities of the United States, with intercontinental rockets, cancels out the superiority of the U.S. strategic air force—and has thereby already established a state of stalemate, or nuclear nullity. Counting on such mutual check on the use of nuclear weapons, the Russians may be emboldened to exploit their great superiority in conventional forces, and to be more venturesome in pursuing their political aims. Thus, they may become more inclined to take the risk of forcing a solution of the German problem, before the West German forces are provided with nuclear weapons—feeling that the chances are better at the moment, and the risks less, than they would be if the issue were to be deferred any longer.

While the Russians now have this sense of urgency, the experience of the past ten years has encouraged the Allies to feel that a crisis will subside if they put off any action, while remaining firm in attitude. Such trust in " brinkmanship " might too easily prove misplaced and fatally out of date, if pursued indefinitely—without due regard to the changed circumstances. For some of Kruschev's remarks suggest that he is more ready to carry matters nearer to the brink, in a clearer way, and has thought out methods of doing this that would present the Allies with the fateful decision to " start shooting ".

What could the Allies do if the routes of access to West Berlin are closed ? Their only apparent choice is between trying to force open the roads with an armoured column,

145

and trying to circumvent the barrier by maintaining supplies with an air lift, as they did in 1948.

This brings us face to face with the question how the other side could block the routes of approach, and whether it could do so without opening fire—thus placing the onus of violence on the Western Allies.

The land routes to Berlin from West Germany traverse a hundred miles or more of East Germany territory. This long stretch is intersected with rivers and numerous streams, while the roads run through several expanses of forest. If an Allied armoured column crossed the border the bridges could be blown up successively as it approached. Trees could be felled beforehand and quickly laid across the road when needed. Sections of the road could be blown up and made unusable—all the more easily because the *autobahn* often runs along high embankments. Where it is flatter, concrete blocks and other obstacles could be placed beforehand along the edges to hinder any attempt to move off the road and by-pass the blocked sections. All such obstacles could be passively manned by troops, so that the Allied column could not clear away an obstacle without running over them or opening fire. River-banks might be similarly lined to hinder the laying of bridges.

President Eisenhower showed no realisation of these possibilities, and the other side's scope for passive obstruction, when he said that if the Allies " were stopped, somebody else would be using force " and that " shooting, if there was to be any, could come in the first instance only from the Russian side ". For, in the very nature of the case, it is the side that wants to move forward which has to take violent measures, and start shooting if it is blocked by obstruction.

Once the Allied column started shooting, to clear its path, the Russians—with their twenty mechanised divisions to reinforce the seven East German—could bring into action a

146

strength far exceeding what the West has available. They could easily repulse any Allied attempt to drive on. If the Allies then unleashed tactical nuclear weapons in the hope of disrupting the Russians' concentration of force, the Russians could reply in kind—and the Allied forces, being the ones that were trying to advance in the open, would be the more vulnerable.

If the Allies extended the range of their nuclear bombardment, to the Russian communications, the Russians would be likely to turn their bombardment onto the Anglo-American seaport bases in Europe—which are easier to hit, and more vulnerable, than the Russians' overland lines of supply.

At each stage it would lie with the Allies to raise the stakes, and take the risk of going a stage further—on the fatal course culminating in the strategic nuclear bombardment, and mutual destruction, of each side's centres of population and industry. That is a process which at each stage would tend to operate increasingly to the disadvantage, and ruin, of the more highly organised and civilised countries.

Thus the scheme of launching an armoured force on the road to Berlin, in the hope that such a show of determination would make the Russians give way, looks like a fatally foolish idea. It would be likely to meet an early check, and leave the Allies only the choice between a humiliating retreat or plunging into greater disaster.

As to the idea of overcoming the blockade by an air lift, it looks hardly more promising. For this, too, is a course that the Russians could effectively block without having to " start shooting ". West Berlin is a small area, and could be ringed with a balloon barrage, hoisted in the adjoining East German territory. That would block the gliding path approach to the Allied airfields in West Berlin. It could be supplemented by parachute-and-cable curtain devices similar to those which were used in World War II as an additional deterrent to

147

low-flying attack on factories. Obstructive patrolling and
"buzzing ", might also be practised in the three air corridors
to Berlin from the West. An air lift could hardly be maintained under such hindrances.

The basic facts of the Berlin problem are that the Russians
stand in an impassable position and the Allies in an impossible one—only tenable as long as Russia lets them keep the
tenancy of the cell in which they foolishly locked themselves
in 1945. Their present troubles flow from the shortsighted-
ness and unrealism of the American and British Governments then in agreeing to a distribution of occupation zones
which gave them no direct access to Berlin, and this put their
position in pawn. Roosevelt, Truman, and Eisenhower,
Churchill and Attlee, share the responsibility for that stu-
pendous folly.

The Allies' best hope now lies not in continual procrastina-
tion, but in seeking to negotiate a wider arrangement for
reducing tension, on the lines of mutual withdrawal—thereby
making possible their own extrication from the Berlin dilemma, and trap. Having delayed so long while their disadvantages were growing, they are in a poor position for
bargaining. But their best support may be, with the calculating Russians, the reflection that opponents who blindly put
themselves at such a disadvantage in 1945 may be mad
enough to commit themselves to a suicidal war rather than
surrender a disadvantageous position under threat. Kruschev
would be wise to realise the danger of moves that produce
violent emotional reactions.

14

CLOUD OVER THE BALTIC FLANK

WHEN NATO was born, it was conceived primarily with the idea of covering the west of Europe against a Russian invasion, and the main military effort has gone into building up a shield force on what is called the Central Europe front. Subsequently, after Greece and Turkey became members in 1952, the second concern became to build up a shield for the southern front and flank of NATO, in the Mediterranean area. By comparison, little attention has been given to NATO'S northern flank, although Denmark and Norway have been members since the start, and very little has been done towards creating a shield force in this area.

This northern flank is NATO'S weakest spot in Europe— and in every sense. It is the weakest in actual forces available for defence, the weakest in strategical vulnerability, and the weakest in organisation. Such a combination of glaring weaknesses is enough to make any realist shudder.

It carries a grave danger to the Central Europe front, which could be outflanked in this way. But the southern members of NATO in the Mediterranean would also suffer from the effects of a penetration and collapse of the northern flank. For Denmark and Norway cover the ocean outlets of Soviet Russia's large force of fast and long-range submarines, the major part of which is stationed in the Baltic and Arctic ports.

This does not necessarily mean, as is still commonly assumed by many admirals of the older school, that Russia's submarines would be used for a blockade similar to what was seen in the last two world wars—an unlimited sink-at-sight campaign. The very fact that such a blockade would be a *vital* threat—particularly to Britain, because of her dependence on seaborne supplies for feeding her population— makes it unlikely that Russia's rulers would venture to launch a campaign of this kind unless they were prepared to risk all-out war. For in that event a submarine campaign would be superfluous, since it is inherently a slow way of producing decisive results. But Russia's submarines could be used, in a more subtle way, for a hindrance campaign of great nuisance effect—imposing costly precautions and an exhausting strain on NATO sea-traffic, military and mercantile.

The Russian submarine forces in the Baltic are at present strategically restricted because, except by slow passage along internal waterways, they can only reach the high seas by passing through the very narrow straits (barely four miles wide) between Denmark and southern Sweden—or between the Danish islands of Zealand and Funen—and then through the still narrow channels of the Kattegat and Skaggerak, between Danish Jutland and Southern Norway. In the course of the passage from the Baltic to the North Sea, they have to traverse three hundred miles of restricted waters.

If this bottleneck were to be uncorked, the ninety or more submarines of Russia's Baltic Fleet would be able to get out onto the Atlantic and harass all the ocean routes to Western and Southern Europe. They could operate against any part of these routes, even off the American coast itself, or inside the Mediterranean Sea. For the possible range of action, or surface endurance, of what are now classified as medium range submarines is from 4,000 to 8,000 miles, while that of the new W and Z classes is 12,000 miles and more.

The Baltic could be all too easily uncorked. Besides the

weakness of the forces covering the Danish outlet, the defensive position there is inherently weak from a strategical point of view. That basic fact was impressed on my mind in 1933, when I visited Denmark just after Hitler came to power, and was consulted by the Danish Commander-in-Chief about the plans for the defence of Denmark against a German attack. After a survey of the strategical problem and the lines of approach, the most that seemed to me possible was a brief delaying action in the Jutland peninsula in the hope of gaining time until Allied help arrived—and even that would only be possible if adequate preparations were made. It was palpably impossible to hold Zealand, the main island, where Copenhagen lies, and I pointed out how easily the capital could be seized by a surprise coup from the Baltic by sea-borne and airborne forces. The planned defences appeared so futile that I suggested it would be wiser to remove those which existed, drop their extension, and declare Copenhagen an open city.

The forecast and advice were regarded as unduly pessimistic by ardently patriotic Danes. Moreover, their optimistic view was shared, as late as March 1940, by members of the British Government, who argued that it would be strategically advantageous to take an offensive lead in this quarter, bringing Denmark and Norway into the war. Churchill was the foremost advocate of taking the initiative there, and starting such a move. But when the threat provoked Hitler to forestall it, at the beginning of April 1940, the key points of Denmark were captured by surprise within a few hours, and resistance immediately collapsed, while the keypoints of Norway were captured almost as quickly, and although parts of the disjointed Norwegian forces held out long enough for British and French help to arrive on the scene, the rest of the country was overrun and occupied within a few weeks.

It would hardly be more difficult now for the Russians to

151

repeat Hitler's coup. Only an eighty mile stretch of flat country lies between the Russian mechanised forces poised near Lubeck in Germany, and the southern border of the Jutland peninsula. Moreover, the sea approaches to the Sound, the strait between Zealand and Sweden, are just as accessible to the Russian naval forces as they were to the German in 1940. Russia also has much larger airborne forces than Germany had then, and these could be used to seize by surprise both Zealand and Jutland.

For a seaborne attack, like that of the Germans in 1940, the Russian Baltic Fleet has available eight powerful modern cruisers and some forty destroyers, apart from numerous smaller craft, as well as its ninety submarines. The Western forces for the defence of the bottleneck are much weaker. The Danish navy consists of only two destroyers, six frigates, and four submarines. Most of this small force is obsolescent. The Norwegian navy comprises six destroyers, ten frigates, and eight submarines, while the new German navy will before long have twelve, six and twelve respectively—but it is doubtful whether either of these small navies could effectively intervene in time to meet a sudden seaborne attack on the Danish islands that bar the exit from the Baltic.

Denmark has an Army so small that its available forces are barely the equivalent of one division, and even these are not in the state of instant readiness for action that is needed to counter a surprise stroke. For such a stroke, Russia has available some ten airborne divisions, and sufficient air transport to carry two of them in a single lift. Moreover, her advanced striking force in East German territory comprises twenty mechanised divisions, and part of these could be used for an overland thrust into Jutland, while the rest warded off the intervention of NATO'S Northern Army Group—which is numerically weaker, and less fully mechanised.

Cloud Over the Baltic Flank

The difficulty of effective resistance is increased because responsibility for the defence of the Baltic bottleneck is separated from the main Central Europe front, although it covers the immediate flank of this front. The responsibility is entrusted, along with that of Norway's far-stretching territory, to Headquarters, Allied Forces, Northern Europe. But in this high-sounding command the actual forces are tiny compared with those in the other NATO Commands, while the land forces of Denmark and Norway are under separate sub-commands.

Moreover, effective support in emergency is hindered by the unwillingness of these two countries to allow other NATO forces to be stationed there, or bases established there, before an emergency occurs—in order to avoid provoking Russia. Such reluctance is understandable in the circumstances, but it reduces their membership to NATO to the point of absurdity. Unless they are willing to accept the presence of NATO reinforcements, ready in reserve on the spot, it would be more sensible to revert to neutrality, in line with Sweden. Their present attitude tends to combine provocation with temptation—which proved a fatal combination in the case of Poland twenty years ago.

Norway's land forces are no larger than Denmark's— equivalent to one division. They would have little chance of withstanding a Russian airborne pounce upon the south coast of Norway, bordering the Skaggerak outlet from the Baltic. Moreover, that strip, although the most important strategically, is only a small fraction of the immense coastline that Norway has to defend—which is 1,600 miles in length from its junction with Sweden in the Skaggerak to its northern extremity facing Russia's Arctic base at Murmansk. Despite the ruggedness of the country, its defence with such small forces would be an almost hopeless task against the strength that the Russians could deploy. The seizure of the northern stretch of Norway would ease the way for Russia's submarines to get into the Atlantic from their Arctic bases, while the seizure of ports on the Atlantic coast of Norway would enable them to operate more effectively against the NATO supply routes.

When account is taken of the vulnerability of NATO'S northern flank, and the present defencelessness of Denmark and Norway, it is astonishing that so little attention should be given to the risks in this quarter. Complacency about the prospect and the problem is hard to understand.

In the past it has been too readily assumed that any Russian move into Danish or Norwegian territory would automatically produce nuclear retaliation against Russia by the NATO striking forces, and that this counter-threat is sufficient to deter any such move. But with the development of mutual nuclear power, and of long-range missile means of delivery, this becomes very questionable. If the Russians, on some convenient pretext, were to make a sudden pounce to occupy such points, and then immediately offer to negotiate a settlement on the basis of " free passage " rights, to warm waters, would the major Western Powers actually venture to bring on a suicidal all-out war with nuclear weapons rather than negotiate? No area so easily lends itself, to and invites, this kind of twenty-four hour pounce as does the Scandinavian stretch on the northern flank of NATO, especially in its present state of acute weakness.

As Denmark and Norway are so reluctant to have troops from other NATO countries stationed on their soil, the best answer to the danger of such a surprise stroke would be a floating fire brigade—an amphibious force, based on the harbours in Northern Germany or those in the North British islands, which could throw a strong and well-organised reinforcement of marines ashore at short notice.

154

15

CLOUD OVER THE NEAR EAST FLANK

BESIDES Berlin and the Baltic there are other exposed out-post positions, on the flanks of NATO, which would be almost as difficult to defend—and it would be wise to reckon with the possibility that they may become targets of Soviet politico-military strategy.

The most obvious of these precarious positions is Persia, whose territory forms the gateway to the rest of the Middle East. In recent years the situation in Persia has become better, and firmer on the surface at any rate. Unhappily, conditions of instability and combustibility have spread—particularly to the westward and south-westward parts of the Middle East. That has, naturally, prompted intervention—direct or indirect—by outside Powers. It has also offered opportunity to insidious trouble-making for political and strategical advantage.

Renewed Soviet pressure on Persia was ominously fore-shadowed in 1959, when the Soviet Government made a vehement public complaint that the Shah's Government was pursuing a double-dealing policy which could have grave consequences. This note stated that the Persians had made proposals to it for a treaty of friendship and non-aggression, but then suddenly broken off negotiations under American pressure, while arranging a new military pact with the United States.

There is a long background to the present situation, and it is very important to see this in perspective. It has been a prolonged sequence of pull and counter-pull, with Persia as the rope in a veiled tug-of-war.

Thirteen years ago the Shah took a bold step, and a big risk, by clearing out the Communist puppet Government in the frontier province of Azerbaijan, and also suppressing the left-wing Tudeh party in Persia, which was a potential Soviet fifth column. To the world's surprise, Stalin swallowed this double rebuff and took no open counter-action. But in 1950 the Shah's prime minister, General Razmara, was assassinated, and a wave of extreme nationalism brought Dr. Mussadek into power. The Communists and fellow-travellers co-operated with this Nationalist party, and fostered its clamour for taking over the British-owned oilfields. Under this cloak, their own influence revived and spread.

When the British were squeezed out, the Americans came to take an increasing hand in Persian affairs. Their military mission had already, several years earlier, been given exclusive rights to guide the organisation and training of the Persian Army. Behind the scenes they now backed a counter-move by the Shah's supporters, particularly the Army leaders. In 1953 a military-royalist coup overthrew Mussadek's Government, and restored the Shah's power.

Then, in 1955, the Shah's Government joined in the Baghdad Pact—the military alliance of Turkey, Iraq, Persia, Pakistan and Britain for joint defence of the Middle East. The Shah's desire for such a guarantee played an important part in producing this Pact, and in overcoming the doubts felt in the West about its military value and political wisdom —doubts based on the provocative effect of such a military alliance on Russia's southern border, and the tempting effect of its strategic weakness. The Shah's initiative was prompted by reports that British strategists were planning a defence of the Middle East along the line of the mountain chain which covers the northern and western frontiers of Iraq—

which implied abandonment of any attempt to defend Persia.

The Soviet Government loudly protested against Persia's step in signing the Baghdad Pact, as a breach of its long-standing neutrality treaty with Russia. But it abstained, once again, from following up its warning by any direct action. Instead, it resorted to indirect counter-moves. The first of these was the arms deal with Egypt, which helped to develop a paralysing distraction in the rear of the newly-built northward-facing alliance—the northern shield as the Americans call it, or the American spearhead as the Russians regard it.

Nasser's subsequent activities in extending his sway, and undermining British influence in the neighbouring countries, were most effective in serving Kruschev's disruptive purpose. That has been the result, too, of all anti-Western ferment. As has been aptly remarked: " Communism has adopted the language of Arab nationalism as its own."

Then, in July 1958, came the military revolution in Iraq, headed by General Kassem. This automatically disjointed the central link in the Baghdad Pact alliance. The United States Government, which had hitherto held back from full entry into the Pact, immediately reacted by pledging itself to defend the remaining Middle East members—Persia, Pakistan and Turkey. It thus committed itself more definitely and deeply than ever before.

The formulation of a contract was not so quick. But by December it was approaching completion. The Soviet Government then sought to check it by a fresh warning to Persia—that it regarded such an arrangement as an immediate danger to the Soviet Union. It stiffly reminded Persia that the Soviet-Persian treaty of 1921, amplified by that of 1927, gave it the right in case of such danger " to send its army into Persia in order to take the necessary military steps in its own defence ".

Anxiety about this warning, and dissatisfaction with the initial American proposals, may have led the Shah's Government to make its under-cover bid early in 1959 for a fresh treaty with Russia, as a re-insurance. The way it broke off negotiations may have been due to the Russians asking too much, or to the Americans promising more.

But the crucial question remains—what could the Americans do if Russia moved troops into Persia on the pretext of the 1927 treaty?

Persia has a natural defensive shield in her mountainous northern frontier, facing Russia, and the successive mountain chains that lie behind it form a series of barrier positions which provide the basis for a prolonged defence in depth. But the effective value of such barriers depends on having forces strong enough to hold them firmly. They are not in themselves more than a momentary obstacle to mechanised forces. That was made clear in 1941 when the German panzer forces swept through the mountainous Balkans in a few days, overrunning the Yugoslav and Greek armies. Yet these were numerically large armies, composed of tough troops. The way they were so quickly pulverised showed that toughness is not enough, when up-to-date arms and equipment are lacking.

It is all too plain that the Persian Army is weak in all respects, compared with either of those armies. It numbers about 120,000 men, and a nominal thirteen small-scale divisions. In recent years a small amount of relatively modern equipment has been provided from American and other sources, and American officers have helped with instructional guidance. But only four or five of these small divisions can be reckoned effective, and even in these the amount of modern arms and equipment is inadequate. Although three are called " armoured divisions ", their tanks are of obsolescent types. Worse still, there is a scarcity of anti-tank guns.

The pay of the troops is very low, and discontent on this score has made many of the soldiers, and junior officers, susceptible to Communist propaganda. Even if the solidity of the army could be relied on, it would be a very small force to cover the 700 miles stretch of Persia's northern frontier—250 miles to the west of the Caspian Sea, and 450 miles to the east—as well as the 400 miles stretch of her eastern frontier facing Afghanistan.

Under such conditions the best chance of putting a brake on a Russian invasion, apart from nuclear weapons, lies in well-judged demolition on the roads through the mountains. But an extensive network of demolitions requires not only much skill but large resources—both of which are dubious quantities in this area. It is not surprising that some of Persia's own officers, surveying the problem of defence, should have remarked that the Russians would probably overrun the country within a week unless outside help arrives in the first few days, and on a big scale.

A Russian advance into the Middle East would be most likely to come through Persian Azerbaijan and could be continued into Iraq over the passes leading to Rowanduz and Kirkut. That is the shortest route, since it has little more than a hundred miles of Persian territory to traverse before crossing the Iraq frontier. The Russians might use airborne troops to open the way and keep it open.

But we have also to reckon with the possibility of an outflanking thrust into Persia from the area east of the Caspian Sea—by the Russians or by the Afghans, who have been well equipped with Russian material. If they quickly overran Persia they might invade Iraq from other points along the 600 mile stretch of frontier between Rowanduz and the Persian Gulf. That is an immense stretch to cover, even though most of it is mountainous. Iraq, south and west of the frontier, is a wonderful arena for the manoeuvre of

159

armoured forces—and an invader might pour in streams of them, once he had secured the mountain passage ways.

Behind Iraq, or on its rearward flanks, lie Syria, Lebanon, Jordan and Saudi Arabia. None of these States have frontiers that are good for defence against invasion—though desert approaches might help to limit an invader's operational strength.

None of them have forces capable of offering serious resistance to Russian invasion of even such limited strength. Moreover, there is a serious risk that Iraq might serve as a Russian satellite, or at least as a salient.

The only efficient army in the Middle East is that of Israel. In repelling the several-sided invasion from the Arab countries in 1948, and again in its " Hundred Hours " campaign against the Egyptians in 1956, it proved its high quality. It is, clearly, the toughest fighting force in the Middle East, with leaders who are vigorous, militarily well-educated, and highly intelligent—a rare combination. But its strength and equipment are slender for meeting invasion by a Great Power such as Russia.

The Soviet Army has some fifteen well-equipped active divisions poised in the Caucasus, west of the Caspian, and a further nine or ten stationed fairly close, while it could soon double the total with the aid of the three railway lines running up to the front in this strategic area. Thus it has a strength easily capable of overrunning Persia. While it might be difficult for Russia to maintain supplies to a force of more than fifteen divisions in a prolonged advance, to the Persian Gulf, such a force should amply suffice to brush aside the Persian Army and any Allied reinforcements that could be sent to its aid.

The Americans have a large military mission in Persia, but no combat formations anywhere near—only the three battations of Marines with the Sixth Fleet in the Mediterranean.

160

In the Lebanon crisis of 1958 they had to be supplemented by an airborne battle group flown there from the U.S. Seventh Army in Germany. In the United States there is a strategic reserve of four divisions, two of them airborne— but Persia might be overrun before even one of these could arrive on the scene.

The British, since Suez, are little better placed than the Americans to provide early reinforcement, and their strategic reserve is much smaller. The most that they could at present send to the scene quickly is the one parachute brigade which they despatched to Jordan in the 1958 crisis. Its despatch to such a remote theatre as Persia would be a far more difficult problem, both initially and in the maintenance of its supplies.

There is another and numerically stronger piece on the board—Turkey. She stands on the left edge, and her location used to be described as the Near East. That term is still correct, geographically and strategically—because her western frontier lies in Europe, adjoining those of Bulgaria and Greece, so that she is exposed to invasion from that quarter, by the Russians and their Balkan satellites. But her eastern frontier lies in the Middle East, adjoining Persia as well as Russia's Caucasus frontier. Her flanking position in that area is of great strategic importance and influence, potentially.

Britain and France took the lead in making a treaty of mutual assistance with Turkey. That has been reinforced by America's backing, and developed by Turkey's definite incorporation in the framework of Allied defence planning. Nature has provided her land with strong barricades, and these are backed by a standing Army of nearly 400,000 men —organised in some twenty-five divisions, of which about six are of armoured type, although not yet fully equipped, nor adequately modern. The Turks have proved tough fighters in the past—and have more recently shown that

161

again in Korea. The Army is in process of being modernised with American aid. It suffers from growing pains, but should be capable of holding its own in defence—which has always been its strong point.

If Turkey could stretch out an arm quickly enough to help cover her neighbour, Persia, against a Russian thrust from the Caucasus, it would make a great difference to the prospect of initial defence—the most important phase. But whether it could develop an effective counter-offensive outside its own borders is very dubious.

Russia's forces available for use there are vastly larger than those which could oppose her, while her airborne divisions form a means of quickly forcing mountain barriers, seizing keypoints deep in rear, and spreading panic.

The present land defence of the Middle East all too aptly recalls Hans Andersen's fairy-tale entitled " The Emperor's New Clothes ". That was the story of how certain impostors, who knew human weakness, pretended to weave for an Emperor a new suit which, they alleged, had the property of being invisible to everyone who was unfit for his office. The Ministers and the Emperor did not care to admit they could not see it—until a little child exclaimed: " But the Emperor has nothing on at all."

In sum, there seems no chance, or way, of defending Persia against invasion except by the American air forces in the Mediterranean area—and their use of tactical nuclear weapons. That would carry a heavy risk of developing into all-out nuclear war. So there might well be more hesitation in taking the decision to unleash such action than there has been in giving Persia an assurance of protection. Western policy has moved fast in extending its protective embrace to the Middle East. But it has, unfortunately, moved faster and further than the strategic possibilities.

The Polish Guarantee in the spring of 1939 had near-fatal

consequences for all countries concerned. The consequences of a Persian Guarantee in the nuclear age could be far worse. It can only be hoped that Kruschev will be more conscious of this basic fact than the givers of the guarantee—and that he will resist the inclination to exploit its weaknesses better than Hitler did when confronted with the combined provocation and temptation of the Polish Guarantee.

He may well reckon that there is more to gain by pursuing an indirect policy and strategy of subversion than through any direct action in the Middle East by the Russian Army. For it is all too clear that he has abundant scope there for " fishing in troubled waters ". A fresh turn of the revolutionary wheel could bring Communist-dominated parties into power in Iraq, Syria, and elsewhere—or in Persia itself. Such governments might be prompted to call for Russian support, and protective reinforcement, in the same way that the British were called into Jordan on King Hussein's appeal and the Americans into Lebanon by President Chamoun's.

The Russians have the strongest airborne force in the world—some ten airborne divisions, and sufficient air transport probably to carry two of these in a single lift. The sudden arrival of two of these divisions in any of these Middle East countries, at the invitation of its Government, would place the Western Powers in an extremely awkward situation.

Other danger spots in the Middle East are the Aden Protectorate and the oil-bearing States in Southern Arabia, along the Persian Gulf, that are linked with Britain by treaty or directly under British protection. In the spring of 1958, and twice the year before, the British troops at Aden went into action to repel incursions from the Yemen—which has revived the old claim that the Aden Protectorate is part of its historic territory. In 1957, too, a British force was called in by the Sultan of Muscat and Oman to quell a dangerous

163

revolt in his domains, after his own forces had been defeated by the Imam of Oman.

The Aden situation has become more precarious since Russia has been supplying tanks, self-propelled guns, and other arms to the Yemen. Two years ago it was arranged that the Russian engineers should start building a harbour on the Red Sea coast of the Yemen for the establishment of a naval base there.

Trouble might flare up afresh any time, and we have to reckon with the possibility that the Yemenis might be prompted or bribed on the pretext of British aggression, to call on Russian help to protect them. The British in Aden would have a shock if they woke up one morning to find that Russian volunteers had been dropped by air behind the disputed frontier, and were manning the Russian tanks and guns already shipped to the Yemen.

The most essential, while least provocative, precaution against such emergencies would be the offshore presence, on the seas girdling this troubled area, of an amphibious force capable of putting a " fireguard " or " fire extinguisher " ashore quickly. The U.S. Sixth Fleet, with its independence of land bases or airfields, provides such manoeuvrable but unprovocative aid for the eastern end of the Mediterranean —the Near East. It could be more effective still if the scale of its marine component was increased. But there is at present no such amphibious aid available in the Red Sea and Indian Ocean for the Southern Arabia and Persian Gulf area. This is a need which the British could meet if they developed an adequate amphibious force for the purpose.

16

THE DEFENCE OF CENTRAL EUROPE

In calculating the scale of force required for defence, it is necessary to emphasise, and keep in mind, three important qualifications to the evidence about the comparative power of the defensive and the offensive—as a safeguard against over-optimistic estimates of what will suffice.

The first is that the offensive potentially carries one unique advantage—that if the attack is made unexpectedly and with sustained speed of follow-through it may split a slow-responding defence so deeply and disintegratingly as to *paralyse* resistance, annulling the comparative balance of numerical strength. Defence, however effective, can never produce such a catastrophic collapse of the enemy as does this tactical and strategical " fission-effect " of a sustained-speed attack.

The second qualification, arising from the first, is that any calculation of numbers is dependent upon the standard of *performance*. The basic advantage of defence can only be ensured if a defence has adequate flexibility and mobility— the primary condition being that the defender has a clear understanding of the attacker's technique and its tempo. Lack of such understanding was the principal cause of the Allied disasters in 1940. The time factor is of crucial importance in relation to the ratio of force to space.

The third qualification is that the wider that the front is, relative to the forces, the more scope the attacker has for manoeuvre—and thus the more chance to find gaps in the opposing network of fire that he can penetrate. Although on the Eastern Front the Germans often defeated set-piece offensives on sectors where the Russians had concentrated a 7 to 1 superiority of force, the Russians usually succeeded in finding penetrable stretches somewhere on the front when their *overall* superiority had risen to about 3 to 1.

With the NATO forces it would be unwise to reckon that they could hold their own with as low a ratio as that on which the Germans managed to do so—in view of the NATO mixture of nationalities, different training systems, and other handicaps. But if their forces had a ratio of 2 to 3 that should be a safe insurance against a sudden attack, provided that they attain adequate mobility and flexibility. At present they are not adequate in these essential qualities, and this deficiency is more important than lack of numbers.

To have any real chance of repelling a sudden high-speed attack, the " shield force " must be composed of fully mobile divisions, always ready for immediate action, and highly-trained. It is folly to imagine that it would be possible with forces of short-term service, even if their numbers were doubled or trebled. The need cannot be fulfilled unless the shield force is composed of professional troops or long-term conscripts—two years' service would be the minimum for the purpose. It would be best, and probably more economic, that all the divisions in the shield force should consist entirely of long-service Regulars.

The Soviet forces in Eastern Germany comprise twenty mobile divisions. So a NATO strength of about thirteen ready-for-action Regular divisions should be able to check a sudden attack by this force—without resorting to atomic weapons, and without yielding ground. It would be better able to check such an attack than the present NATO shield force of twenty-one divisions, which is handicapped by its large proportion of short-service conscripts.

Intelligence experts reckon that the Soviet forces might

166

possibly be raised to forty divisions within about ten days, although it would not be easy to bring up such a large reinforcement without being detected, and thus giving NATO warning and time for counter-measures. But even if the Soviet striking force was thus doubled, a NATO force of twenty-six Regular divisions should suffice to keep it in check; or alternatively, twenty Regular divisions and a German citizen militia equivalent to ten divisions, organised and trained for static or locally mobile defence.

Such a combination would be a much better shield than the thirty present-type divisions, of short service conscripts mixed with Regulars, that the existing NATO plan aims to achieve. It could be more immediately ready for action, more efficient in performance, and more truly economic.

If any surprise attack was promptly checked, it is unlikely that the incursion would be continued. For its chance of success in producing a *fait accompli* would have vanished, while persistence in it would hour by hour increase the risk of detonating a nuclear war—which would nullify the aggressor's *object*. Moreover, according to authoritative estimates, the maximum strength to which the Soviet force on this front could be built up logistically even after a month is sixty divisions. In defence, a NATO force of forty divisions should suffice to keep that number in check and *without the use of atomic weapons*. Such a strength can be attained within a month of mobilisation even under present NATO arrangements.

So there is a good insurance against the most unlikely contingency of a massive invasion, if the training and organisation of the NATO force matches that of its opponents. The basic requirement is an improvement of quality rather than an increase of quantity.

It may be argued that a shield force on a 2 to 3 ratio, although a good insurance in relation to the Russian forces on the NATO central front, would not be adequate in relation to space—because of the width of that front. So a fuller examination of this aspect of the problem may help to clarify the issue. In such an examination there are two key questions—what is the *tactical minimum* of troops necessary to cover and control a given space, and what is the *strategical minimum*?

The first question turns on a calculation of the extent of space that troops armed with modern weapons, other than nuclear ones, can cover with a closely interwoven network of fire. In examination, it soon becomes evident that the ratio of troops to frontage customary in recent wars, and in conventional military doctrine, does not correspond to the ratio of development in weapons during the last hundred years, and in their capacity to cover an area with a sustained downpour of fire.

Nearly a century ago, in the later stages of the American Civil War, Lee's army kept Grant's greatly superior numbers in check for many months—until its strength fell below 1,500 men to the mile. More than half a century ago the Boers repeatedly succeeded in repelling attacks—by British forces which vastly outnumbered them—with a strength of only 600 to 800 men to the mile. Weapons have developed so immensely since then in range and power, that it is hard to see a reason why the tactical minimum considered necessary and customary in practice, has not been adjusted proportionately.

Is there any reason, other than custom fostered by caution? The surmise that this is the real explanation tends to be confirmed by examination of operations in both the First and Second World Wars. For it is evident that attacks were often checked by small detachments or remnants that were heavily outnumbered—whereas attacks succeeded in many cases where the defenders were far more numerous relatively to the frontage. The contrast suggests that a build-up of the defence, to the level suggested by custom and caution, often aided the attacker by presenting him with a much increased target—easier for him to destroy by concentrated fire.

There is abundant evidence from the last war to show that German divisions of depleted strength often successfully defended frontages of twenty to twenty-five miles (thirty to forty kilometres). There are also some notable examples on the Allied side of similar performances. So it is reasonable to consider a frontage of twenty-five miles (forty kilometres) as within the defensive capacity of a fully mobile division of present strength—as is now coming to be recognised in high military quarters. Taking account of the corps and army troops available to support a division, it represents a basic scale of about 1,000 men to the mile (600 men to the kilometre).

That scale is not much less than what proved adequate for effective defence in the later stages of the American Civil War, and more than the scale with which the Boers maintained their defence nearly sixty years ago. Thus it might be further reducible after a more thorough scientific analysis, of recent war experience and weapon capabilities. Such a re-investigation is very desirable. For a reduction of the *tactical minimum* considered necessary to provide an effective curtain of fire and " control a given space " would reduce the problem of providing the *strategical minimum*—especially in mobile reserves—to maintain a forward defence of the NATO front as a whole.

But for the time being it is safer to take a scale of one mobile division for twenty-five miles (forty kilometres) of front as the *tactical minimum*. On that basis, ten such divisions would be needed to cover the front, between the Baltic and Bohemian mountains, that is threatened by the Russian forces poised in East Germany. Beyond this number

169

adequate mobile reserves should be available to counter-balance the attacker's power—and inherent advantage —of concentrating his effort along a particular line of thrust.

Here we come to the question of the *strategical minimum*. Views on the subject still tend to reflect the habit of thought that developed in World War I, and its doctrinal legacy. The continuous trench-front that came to be established in 1914 on the Western Front, and persisted throughout the war, left a lasting impression. It was deepened by the low mobility of forces at that time. Ever since, there has been a tendency to assume that the whole strength of a frontier ought to be pro-vided with the tactical minimum for effective defence of every sector, both in forward troops and in local reserves for their support. Thus the *strategical minimum* requirement has come to be regarded as basically no different from the *tactical minimum*. It is a view which amounts to visualising the ex-treme case, extremely improbable, of having to meet a heavy attack on all sectors simultaneously—and demanding forces strong enough for defence everywhere. Its influence is ap-parent in suggestions and arguments that, without the use of nuclear weapons, NATO would need a standing force of as much as seventy divisions on its central front, even against Russian forces of lower strength.

Such a view is contrary to the facts and lessons of war experience. In all wars previous to this century, the forces engaged were very small in proportion to the front as a whole —much *smaller* than they became in the last two wars, al-though *denser* on the battlefield. In the wars of the eighteenth and early nineteenth centuries, a battlefield strength of 20,000 men to the mile was normal, yet countries were suc-cessfully defended with a ratio of merely 250 men to the mile, or less, on the front as a whole—a strategical ratio of forces that was barely more than 1 per cent. of the tactical ratio.

(The Note at the end of the Chapter deals in more detail with this evidence from history.)

The capability of covering a wide front with such relatively small forces, while bringing sufficient tactical strength into action against the enemy's strategic line of advance and concentration, came from the ability to make a good appreciation of the enemy's likely routes of advance and objectives, so that adequate forces could be moved thither to bar his path.

It is hard to see any good reason why this should be considered impossible now. The means of information, of intercommunication, and of movement are much better than in the past—and on balance they favour the defending side, increasing its chances of countering the attacker's initial advantage in surprise.

On NATO's central front it should not be too difficult to gauge an attacker's likely objectives and routes of advance. Although that front is 440 miles (700 kilometres) in extent, only the more northerly stretch of some 250 miles (400 kilometres) is suitable for surprise attack *and* rapid advance by the Soviet mechanised divisions in East Germany. Even within that northerly stretch the suitable routes are limited, and the direction of the enemy's effort should become clear once he starts crossing the rivers near the border. So it ought to be possible to check him in the forward *zone*, by timely counter-moves, with a 2 to 3 ratio of forces, if the NATO covering force is composed of fully mobile and highly trained divisions, and is organised with more strategic flexibility.

Analysis of recent war experience tends to show that the higher the ratio of the mobile reserves to the troops holding the forward position the greater is the prospect of defeating a concentrated thrust. In past practice the divisions in mobile reserve, not tied to a particular sector, have often been less than a quarter of the whole force. Analysis of operations suggests that a half of the whole force would be a better pro-portion—even where it entails thinning the forward defence to a hazardous degree.

This is the basis I have adopted in calculation, and from it comes the suggested figure of twenty-six mobile divisions as the NATO requirement for a shield force capable of meeting both the force and space conditions. That number would provide a defence of 2 to 3 ratio against the possibility that the twenty Soviet divisions in East Germany might be raised to forty within ten days. It would also provide NATO with the requisite tactical minimum of ten divisions as forward defence there, and three for a mobile screen along the moun-tainous Czechoslovakian border, with thirteen more as mobile reserves for the front as a whole. That would be a reasonably good insurance against sudden attack in any direction.

The required number of divisions would be somewhat less if there was a citizen militia, of the Swiss type, available to man a deep network of defence posts in the forward zone—as a means of helping to delay the enemy's advance while the divisions of the mobile reserve converged upon the threa-tened sector. This militia would need to be so organised that the posts could be manned at short notice by militiamen living or working nearby. It would also be desirable to have such a militia available in the rear areas as a check on an enemy airborne descent to seize key-points there and block the countermoves of the NATO mobile divisions.

If a militia force of this kind was available for local defence the requirement for the main shield force might be reduced from twenty-six to twenty divisions—that is, a 1 to 2 basis versus the enemy's possible maximum in a *surprise* offensive on the Central Europe front.

The more northerly stretch of some 250 miles embraces the front from the Baltic to the valley of the Frankische Saale

172

inclusive—so that a forward defence of the suggested scale (ten divisions) would not only cover the northern plain of Germany, but go well round the westward bulge of Thuringia, and cover the routes to Frankfurt across the Thuringer Wald.

Behind that end of the main front is posted the bulk of the U.S. Seventh Army, and it would be natural to continue such a disposition of the mobile reserves—ready to counter a thrust either towards the valley of the Main, and Frankfurt, or into Bavaria. So there would be a good insurance against a circuitous approach by the Russians across the Thuringia-Bavaria frontier. Moreover, such a dog-leg move—first southward and then westward—would entail a loss of time, and diminish the Russians' chances of sustaining the speed-surprise required for success in a sudden coup. Another drawback from the Russians' point of view, is that Bavaria offers no objectives comparable in importance *and* accessibility with those between Frankfurt and the Baltic.

NOTE

EXAMPLES FROM THE WARS OF THE EIGHTEENTH AND NINETEENTH CENTURIES (WHEN WEAPONS WERE OF VERY SHORT RANGE, AND DEFENSIVE CAPABILITY DEPENDED MAINLY ON MOBILITY).

War of the Spanish Succession

In 1709–13, when the French were on the defensive, they had a field force averaging only about 100,000 men to cover their frontier of some 400 miles (i.e. 250 men to the mile *strategically*).

Seven Years' War

In the early stages, 1756–7, Frederick the Great covered his southern front of some 400 miles with about 100,000 men (i.e. 250 men to the mile *strategically*)—against enemy forces double his strength.

Later the enemy coalition brought its total forces in the field up to nearly 400,000, while his total rarely exceeded 150,000 (and diminished from losses during each year's campaign). With that total strength he had to cover an all-round frontage of some 1,500 miles (i.e. 100 men to the mile *strategically*). Although suffering several bad reverses, offsetting his riposte successes, he succeeded in holding out until the enemy coalition dissolved in 1763.

Napoleonic Wars

In 1814, when Napoleon was thrown on the defensive after his defeat in the Battle of Leipzig, he had only 70,000 men to cover his 400-mile front in the north and north-east (i.e. 180 men to the mile *strategically*). The Allied armies which crossed the Rhine to invade France amounted to 370,000 men—more than five times his strength. Yet he succeeded in keeping them in check for three months.

During this period he inflicted nine sharp reverses on them before fate turned against him—when an intercepted letter revealed his plan, of moving round onto their communications, and thus encouraged them to move down the temporarily open path into Paris, where their arrival produced the collapse of his régime.

American Civil War

From 1861 to 1864 the Confederates covered a front of 800 miles between the Atlantic and the Mississippi with a field force averaging about 200,000 men (i.e. 250 to the mile *strategically*)—and kept at bay an enemy double their strength.

The fact that it was possible to maintain an effective defence of a wide front with a *strategical ratio* of only 250 men to the mile, or less, is all the more significant because the *tactical ratio* for effective defence, in open country, was considered to be about 20,000 men to the mile (including local reserves) with the short-range weapons (smooth-bore muskets and cannon) of the Napoleonic Wars and earlier, and about 12,000 to the mile with the improved weapons of the mid-nineteenth century.

The immense difference between the *tactical* (battlefield) ratio and the *strategical* (whole front) ratio shows that the crucial factor in the defence of any wide front is the *time* factor. This turns not only on the relative mobility of the attacking and defending forces, but on the defender's correct appreciation of the attacker's lines of advance. And also on the degree in which the attacker's mobility is cramped—by natural obstacles, fortifications, and counter-threat.

PART FOUR

TACTICAL

17

NEW TACTICS AND TACTICAL ORGANISATION

FOR effective defence, the organisation and tactics of the NATO armies need to be given not only a common shape but a newer shape. Tactics and tactical organisation still follow too closely their 1944-45 pattern. The Allies' success in the final year of the war has led to undue satisfaction with the methods then practised, and until recently there was little change in or re-examination of them. That was the more perilous because the methods were evolved under conditions where the Allies were sure of an overwhelming superiority in air cover, whereas they would now have to meet heavy adverse odds on the ground multiplied by adverse odds in the air. Their methods took too little account of the difficulties of operating under constant menace from the enemy's superior air force. It would be folly to expect that troops could move in anything like as large bodies or use the roads in the same way as in 1944-45. It would become fatal with the development of atomic weapons.

The war clouds that hang over Europe have, however, a " silver lining ". Examination of German experience in 1944-45 is far more encouraging, for the members of NATO, than is apparent from the surface of events—and all the more so because the ground and air odds against the Germans at that time were much worse than the NATO forces now face.

The course of the Second World War created the impression that, in contrast to the experience of the First World

War, attack had become superior to defence in land warfare. Such an impression was an illusion arising from the surface of events.

In 1940 the West was overrun, and the course of history changed, by the German armoured forces, applying a new *Blitzkrieg* technique of swiftly manoeuvring concentration exploited by deep strategic penetration. Guderian, the creator and leader of these " Panzer troops ", stated in his memoirs that their organisation and technique were inspired by my theories and writings of the nineteen-twenties. But in the 1930s I came to see how this revolutionary offensive technique could be countered by a new defensive one. Unfortunately, it proved difficult to induce the French and British General Staffs either to recognise the power of the new offensive technique or to develop the counter-technique. As the new-style attack was met in 1940 by old-style defence, it naturally had the best chance of succeeding, and the result was made the more certain by the Germans' great superiority in the air—particularly in airpower available to support the attack on land. But once Germany's opponents began to develop suitable defensive tactics, and more adequate air support, the *Blitzkrieg* offensive suffered increasing checks.

The exhaustion of Germany's strength in pursuing the offensive coincided with the ever-growing output of arms from her opponents' factories, based on material resources which far exceeded those of Germany and her allies. That material superiority was so great that it ensured the defeat of Germany and her allies once the initial onslaughts were checked.

After the tide of the war had thus been turned, the initial false impression—of the basic superiority of attack over defence—was renewed by the superficial appearance of the Allied campaigns as an unbroken " advance to victory ", punctuated only by occasional halts.

But in deeper examination and analysis of the operations it becomes evident that Allied attacks rarely succeeded unless the attacking troops had a superiority in strength of *more than 5 to 1*, accompanied by domination of the air. On the Eastern Front the Russian attacks had still higher ground odds, though less air strength. There, again, the attacks were repeatedly held up unless they had ample space for outflanking the defence.

In the Normandy campaign of 1944 there was much less room for manoeuvre than on the Eastern Front, and the course of the struggle was very significant in the way it showed the power of skilful defence to hold up a greatly superior attacker. On the British front the most striking case of all was " Operation Bluecoat "—the attempted break-out southward from Caumont on July 30. Here the stroke was so well conceived, and the westward switch from the Caen sector so well organised, that it succeeded in concentrating and launching two specially strong army corps against a ten-mile sector held by only two weak German infantry regiments. The attackers' superiority in fighting units was nearly *10 to 1*, and in number of troops was more than that. Being backed by air supremacy, the real measure of advantage must be reckoned as at least 20 to 1, and may well be reckoned as 30 to 1. Moreover, a total of well over 1,000 tanks were concentrated, in this case, on a sector where there were no German tanks in the earlier phase of the battle. Yet the massive blow failed to overcome the thin defence except on the western part of the sector, and even there it was checked on the third day when meagre tank reinforcements began to arrive on the German side. And it suffered continuous checks during the days that followed. Such a sequel to an ably-planned attack tends to show that the defence had inherently a greater superiority over attack than was ever realised.

THE RATIO OF FORCES

If the attacking side requires even a shade of superior strength to overcome the defender—a mere 11 to 10—such a requirement really shows that, materially, defence is superior to attack.

This simple issue and test had been confused by cases where an attacker inferior in strength has (*a*) met a defender much weaker in morale; or (*b*) had space for manoeuvre, and the skill to exploit it. Military thought, in treating the question of attack and defence, has not yet learned to discriminate clearly between offensive *manoeuvre* and direct *attack*.

The British General Staff, however, showed a notable growth of realism when, after four years' war experience, they issued a new " Umpiring " manual for use in training which laid down that, to succeed in an *attack*, a 3 to 1 superiority of strength was normally required. This calculation corresponds to the ratio deduced from the experience of World War I and set forth in the British Official History, and also that which the German General Staff had taken as a working guide between the wars. The question remains whether a 3 to 1 ratio fully represents the basic superiority of defence over attack in the light of World War II experience.

Fifteen years have passed since the war ended, yet the significance of the comparative odds in Normandy, in relation to the results, has never been adequately brought out in any official report, history, or training manual. There has been too much glorification of the campaign and too little objective investigation. The detailed accounts of the campaign hitherto produced have been " missing the wood for the trees ".

In the light of the basic data already brought out, it is evident that the resistance capacity of an efficient and determined defence has been under-estimated, and is potentially greater than has yet been recognised in staff studies or military doctrine. So there is much value to be gained from a closer study of the defence mechanism in the 1944–45 battles, and of the technique which the Germans applied.

DEFENCE TECHNIQUE

The German defensive tactics in Normandy and later were a blend of static defence with dynamic defence by dispersed battle-groups—making sharp " finger-thrusts ". These repeatedly checked the Allied columns and brought them gradually to a halt, not usually on any pre-chosen line. (We still talk about fighting the " main battle " on some river line. The " main battle ", it seems to me, is an out-of-date concept.) By contrast with the effect of the multiple finger-thrusts, the German attempts at concentrated counter-attack failed repeatedly, and almost invariably, under Allied air and artillery action.

On the Russian Front the defensive capacity of small mobile forces, distributed in battle-groups and skilfully handled, proved even more remarkable. Panzer divisions, even when much under strength, often successfully covered twenty-mile frontages against heavy odds for several weeks, yielding very little ground. Another point which emerges is that the German defence was most effective whenever it could throw the Russians out of their stride—and least effective whenever the Russians were able to mount a *deliberate* attack, particularly an attack on a river line.

In sum, examination of experience in the last war is far more encouraging to the prospects of defence than is apparent from the surface of events. Analysis reveals that prolonged resistance can be achieved by forces that are heavily outnumbered if the tactics of mobile defence, by delaying action combined with riposte, are properly understood and applied—and tactical organisation developed to fit such tactics.

Tactical

Brilliant as was the performance of the German Panzer forces in 1940, and tremendous as were its results, they were only made possible by the Allies' incompetence and their weakness in the air. In particular the *concentrated* action of armoured divisions was *potentially* out of date by the time it was so successfully put into practice. It is now definitely out of date. There is fatal folly in dreaming that armoured divisions can operate in mass and deliver concentrated punches under an enemy-dominated sky—or in face of atomic weapons.

We need to grasp the principle of " fluidity of force " in contrast to the old and obvious interpretation of " concentration "—and to develop a new technique of *controlled dispersion*. The embryo was contained in German practice during the later years of the war. Indeed, it had been conceived in Britain before the war and was practised by the pioneer tank brigade under Hobart in the trial exercises of 1934.

On the Russian front in 1944–45 the Germans often achieved an amazingly prolonged resistance against much superior numbers, with armoured divisions that were flexibly spread in small combat groups on a wide frontage—twenty miles or more per division. The composition of such groups was usually a battalion of tanks, a battalion of mechanised infantry, and an equivalent artillery unit of self-propelled guns. The units were nearly always below strength.

On the Western Front, too, remarkable delaying and defensive power was produced by similar groups—which, in many cases, were even smaller. Often they were composed of a tank company, a mechanised infantry company, and a battery or two. The tiny scale of such groups was dictated not only by the scanty strength available to cover the large front, but by the better chance they had of evading the ubiquitous and overwhelmingly strong Allied air forces—and by their

182

greater ability to penetrate between the Allied columns and deliver a quick counter-thrust at the most effective moment.

To distribute an armoured division in such a flexible chain of small groups, each of them completely mobile, is essentially different from distributing armour piecemeal to support ordinary infantry—and free from the drawbacks of that practice.

The division, or even the large brigade group, would become a more operable hand if divided into four or five combat groups sub-divided into a similar number of fingers, or minor combat groups, capable of operating separately and practised in doing so. They could, at any moment, be brought together to make a concentrated punch if opportunity arises and air conditions permit. More often still, they could deliver converging stings.

Controlled dispersion is basically different from distribution piecemeal. Little groups thus directed can have multiple effect while not offering concentrated targets to the air. A swarm of hornets do not concentrate—they attack you from all directions simultaneously. That is multiple effect—and should be our guiding idea in applying tactics of controlled dispersion. This kind of multiple envelopment was seen even in Napoleon's campaigns. It was only in his later years that he concentrated before a battle. Earlier he used to keep his numerous small columns coming in from all directions, and they hit the enemy from all directions, each reacting on the other.

The aim of the new tactics must be to *paralyse* the enemy's action. The slogan of " destroying him " in battle leads to self-exposure, self-pinning, and the risk of being smashed. Dominating areas is going to count more than capturing or maintaining positions. We want a new principle of offensive fluidity of force—to operate like the sea or like a swarm of hornets, not like a battering ram. Even in 1940 the decisiveness

183

of the Panzer thrusts of Guderian lay in producing paralysis after penetration, not in producing destruction of the enemy's forces in battle. It really eliminated battle. In Africa Rommel applied such new methods offensively *and* defensively. So did Manteuffel and others on the Eastern Front.

More consideration, too, should be given to what I would call " preparatory tactics and strategy ". A defender has a basic advantage in the fact of being on the spot, before any invasion comes, and occupying the ground over which it would advance. That enables him to reconnoitre routes beforehand for counter-thrusts so that these can be made almost entirely across country. He can also go further than reconnoitre routes. He can prepare those routes, having thought out his moves. He can clear gaps in obstacles so as to make cross-country movement more possible. He can place supplies beforehand in concealed dumps so that the counter-attack forces can move with a minimum of transport. The defender, too, has a potential advantage over the attacker in the way of preparation for moving across rivers without being canalised by the usual bridge limitations. Counter-manoeuvre, properly thought out, has numerous advantages over an invader.

These methods fit the conditions of warfare wherever operations are liable to interruption from the air. They are even better fitted to the conditions of warfare with nuclear weapons—being far less susceptible to breakdown, under such conditions, than present military methods and organisation.

18

TANKS AND THEIR FUTURE

HAS the tank a future—or is it finished ? Can it still play an important part in the military field—if so, what kind of part, and what kind of tank ?

Time after time during the past forty years the highest defence authorities have announced that the tank is dead, or dying. Each time it has risen from the grave to which they had consigned it—and they have been caught napping.

Here are five examples of such death-sentences, recorded in my files. In 1928, when the world's first experimental armoured force was disbanded by the British War Office after two years' trial, an official spokesman declared to the Press that " tanks are no longer a menace ". In 1932 the head of the Historical Section of the Committee of Imperial Defence, General Edmonds, confidently assured me in a letter that : " Any tank which shows its nose in the open ... will be knocked out at once. ... The wars you and Fuller imagine are past."

In 1934 the British Secretary of State for War, Mr. Duff Cooper, predicted that in a few years' time " the most heavily armoured tanks " would be as vulnerable to the new anti-tank weapons as " an old wooden caravan ". A year later the Germans, disregarding his warning, formed their first three panzer divisions—and five years after that the defences of the West were overrun by the tank drive that Guderian led.

The sweeping victory of these armoured forces momentarily opened the eyes of Britain's leaders to the practical value of the new theory that had been conceived there but neglected by them. They belatedly began to build armoured divisions like the Germans. A similar effect was produced on America's leaders.

Even so, the cry that the tank was in decline arose afresh whenever tanks met a temporary check. The cry became particularly strong after the campaign in Sicily and southern Italy, when the mountainous country normally cramped armoured mobility. That affected the preview of its potentialities in the 1944 invasion of France. Churchill had one of his periodical reactions, and in February declared: " We have too much armour—tanks are finished."

His doubts were fanned by his official advisers. The Chief of the Imperial General Staff, Field-Marshal Sir Alan Brooke, addressed a conference of British and American generals, and there sounded a keynote that warfare was back to 1918, and lightning drives of the 1940 kind no longer possible. The U.S. High Command was affected by this slow-motion view.

Yet a few months later, the American and British armoured forces, breaking out from the Normandy bridgehead, drove swiftly forward to within close reach of Germany unchecked by the enemy. Unfortunately, they were then halted by shortage of fuel supplies, due to lack of administrative preparedness to exploit the great opportunity. If there had been more foresight on the top level, the war would have ended that year.

Five years after the war, many top-level soldiers in America and Britain were talking in just the same way as before. On the eve of the Communist invasion of South Korea in 1950, the U.S. Secretary of the Army voiced their views in predicting that: " tank warfare as we have known it will soon be obsolete ". But immediately afterwards the defence of South Korea crumpled under the impact of a small number of obsolescent tanks.

Now, a decade later, another wave of disparagement has arisen—inspired by the belief that the new anti-tank guided missiles have " sounded the death-knell of the tank ". This belief is at least dubious, and could be very precarious—for any army which discards tanks to fight the enemy's tanks, in favour of guided missiles either manually controlled or guided into the target by a " homing " system device.

These missiles are bulky and heavy compared with the shells fired by a tank, thus limiting the amount of ready ammunition that can be carried, while the homing kind are liable to interference and electronic counter-measures. Guided missiles are slow in response and flight compared with the gun in a tank, thus giving the attacker who has a large number of tanks more chance of swamping a defence which relies on missiles to stop them.

The low speed of response and flight allows the enemy tanks sufficient time to move into cover before the missile arrives—behind a tree, hedge, hayrick, house, mound or slope. A tank that is firing from a hull-down position has only to reverse a few yards to get under cover, and become invulnerable. Moreover, the relative slowness of response by the missile gives the tank a good chance of knocking out the launcher before it can shoot. The technique of tank gunnery has developed immensely since 1945 in its combination of speed and precision—so much that it amounts to a new technical break-through.

This striking development in tank gunnery is a fresh re-inforcement of the inherent value of tanks compared with other arms. The basic factors, and most distinctive features, in tank operations are *speed* and *flexibility*. These twin qualities are of more fundamental importance than the armour of the tank. They give its armament, which is not in itself unique, a unique quality in action.

These twin qualities remain essential, and have even

gained in importance, with the coming of nuclear weapons. For the strategic problems of the present time, in a world that lies under the shadow of the catastrophic nuclear cloud, depend more than ever on the time-factor—throughout the whole range of risks from a minor brushfire outbreak or sudden local pounce upwards to all-out war. At every stage, and every level of command, the prospects depend on alertness, on immediate readiness for action, on manoeuvrability in switching forces, and on rapidity of intervention—a combination of requirements embraced in a fuller definition of the twin qualities of speed and flexibility. Such a combination of qualities is essential not only for military success but, above all, for averting the fatal spread of a local outbreak into a world conflagration.

These qualities were not widespread enough among the commanders of armoured forces in World War II—too many of whom had been too long trained in the more deliberate tactics and slower motion of the older arms. In analysing the operations during the war it becomes evident that many reverses and missed opportunities were caused by decisions and orders failing to keep pace with events, and that this failure was due to slowness and rigidity in operational technique.

The most glaring example was the breakdown of the French defence in 1940, following the German armoured forces' thrust across the Meuse. But there were numerous other cases later—in the North African and subsequent campaigns. Moreover, after leaving the desert and re-entering Europe, the difficulties of the ground in Sicily and Italy led the armoured forces to become excessively road-bound, and the habit persisted in north-west Europe even when the opportunities of cross-country movement increased. Another fault was piecemeal action, and particularly the piecemeal distribution of tanks to support infantry—thereby inviting defeat in detail when the opponent was skilful in varying his line of thrust and quick in achieving sudden concentrations of his armour.

There was also a tendency to be too reserve-minded, and to retain so large a proportion of the force in hand as a reserve that the battle took a decisively adverse turn before it was thrown in. That tendency was largely due to habits of thought developed in slow-motion warfare with infantry formations, which when once committed cannot be easily shifted, and a failure to grasp the flexible capacity of an armoured force for disengaging and switching elsewhere—so that even when engaged in one area it is available as a potential reserve for intervention in another if required.

This flexible capacity was significantly demonstrated as far back as 1931, when a tank brigade was formed, in Britain, for a trial of the new ideas about the use and effect of a force composed of fast-moving armoured fighting vehicles. Previous trials had been organised in 1927 with the first Experimental Mechanised Force—but, unfortunately, they were entrusted to a pedestrianly-minded commander, and proved so disappointing that they were abandoned the following year. After a lapse of three years, the General Staff were persuaded to sanction a fresh trial, in 1931, and to put it under an able tank-trained commander, Charles Broad. He wisely started by concentrating on the elementary points that were essential to manoeuvrability. The training technique then adopted helped to pave the way for further progress in time-saving methods of control in manoeuvre. A battle-drill was developed for quick action in carrying out the new tactics of indirect approach and variable thrust that had been advocated and were now adopted.

The financial crisis of that autumn, however, intervened to reinforce cautiously conservative doubts about this new kind of force, and three years passed before a tank brigade was created as a permanent part of the Army, in 1934. Fortunately, command of it was given to another man of vision, Percy Hobart, and striking progress was made. Radiotelephony control was developed for the acceleration of the new tactics, and the exercises that year in southern England saw the first demonstration in practice of the concept of deep strategic penetration by such forces.

The concept was, in brief, that a fast-moving armoured force, operating independently ahead of the main mass of an army, would be capable of carrying out a long-range drive to cut the enemy's communications far back, where his main arteries of supply could be severed. Thus his whole army, and power of resistance, might be paralysed.

The idea had come to my mind initially from studying the long-sustained drives carried out by Genghis Khan's all-mobile forces in the thirteenth century, when the Mongols first swept eastward over China and then turned westward to overrun not only the Middle East but the eastern half of Europe. The concept of modernised " mongol " operations was made a keynote in the training of Britain's first experimental armoured force, and also caught the imagination of General MacArthur, who emphasised it in his 1935 report as Chief of Staff of the United States Army. But I came to see more clearly its application against modern mass armies, dependent on railroads for supply, as a result of studying the Western campaigns of the American Civil War for my book on Sherman in 1929. A blend of the lessons of Sherman's march through Georgia and the Carolinas, which cut off Lee's supplies, and of Forrest's hamstringing raids on the other side provided me with a basis in working out the technique of " deep strategic penetration " for armoured forces.

The subsequent history of the tank has been a story of the prolonged struggle between the original view of the tank as an aid to the infantry assault and the newer view of it as an independent mobile arm. Even after the success of the tests in 1934, the heads of the British Army frowned on such an idea, while also deferring the creation of an armoured division for a further three years.

In 1937–38, when I was for a year the personal adviser of the new Secretary of State for War, Mr. Hore-Belisha, I urged that the British military effort should be concentrated on producing armoured divisions, particularly " because of their value for rapid and powerful riposte in emergency, if a break should be made in the French frontier defences ". Mr. Hore-Belisha himself grasped the point, but the proposal was hotly resisted by the military chiefs. Only two divisions were formed—one at home and one in Egypt—by the time war came in 1939.

Meanwhile, unfortunately, the potentialities of such new-type divisions were more quickly recognised abroad. The Germans, impressed by the British experiment, formed three in 1935, and six by 1939.

Moreover, the idea and technique of deep strategic penetration were enthusiastically embraced by General Guderian, who played the leading part in the creation and training of the German armoured forces. Many of the senior generals in Germany were as sceptical as those in Britain, doubting the possibility of such long-range thrusts and seeing only the hazards. They wanted to tie down the new armoured divisions to the service of the infantry mass. But when war came, opportunity came—to cut loose from their cautious restraints.

The swift conquest of Poland provided proof of the new theory, and dominated the higher command's tendency to impose checks upon its application. When the campaign in the West was launched, Guderian seized the bit in his teeth and bolted with the reins—his unchecked gallop from Sedan to the sea cut off the whole left wing of the opposing armies. The Belgians collapsed, the British barely escaped by sea, and a large part of the French Army was put in the bag. The armoured forces were then quickly switched south and east for a fresh stroke. After the new French front on the Aisne had been pierced, Guderian's sweep eastward to the Swiss frontier cut off the right wing of the French Army, and led to the fall of France. In each case the break-through itself only opened the way for a solution of the problem ; the rapid and deep exploitation was the decisive part.

In the last year or two before the war, the military chiefs of France and Britain were predominantly anti-tank. They even convinced Mr. Churchill, who had fought so hard for the tank in the first war. That had a very unfortunate effect both on the trend of his pre-war efforts to press rearmament, and on his action in the crisis of 1940. He did not grasp the pace of the new tank warfare. When the French Prime Minister telephoned him the news of the break-through made by Guderian at Sedan, Churchill reassuringly replied : " All experience shows that the offensive will come to an end after a while. I remember March 21, 1918. After five or six days they have to halt for supplies." Churchill, like the French military chiefs, was still living in the past. In his memoirs he frankly says : " I did not comprehend the violence of the revolution effected since the last war by the incursion of a mass of fast-moving heavy armour. I knew about it, but it had not altered my inward convictions as it should have done." This state of incomprehension on the Allied side paved the way for Guderian's rapid drive to the Channel coast, which led to Dunkirk and the downfall of France.

The armoured forces that triumphed in 1940 were of primitive composition—as Guderian himself and his fellow tankmen quite realised. They were limited by the means then available and their model was less advanced than the design which had been projected in Britain during the nineteen-twenties. But it sufficed to disrupt the opposing armies

192

because the heads of these armies did not understand the new technique, and were too slow in reacting to moves carried out in " tank-time ".

A similar disruption was achieved the following year, 1941, when the Germans invaded Russia. But as the Germans advanced deeper the inadequate mechanisation of their so-called armoured divisions became an increasing handicap—Russia's poor roads proved a greater obstacle, especially in bad weather, than her tank forces. The number of tanks in the division were too few, and the other components were too lacking in capacity for movement across country, off the road, to by-pass obstacles and resistance. The natural result was that the German panzer attacks became decreasingly effective.

When the tide of the war turned, as the balance of material strength changed in favour of Germany's opponents, on all fronts, there was no comparable revival, and development, of the technique of tank warfare on their side. Few of the higher commanders—American, British, or Russian—had studied the technique of handling armoured formations. They tended to employ their increasing volume of tanks in a multiplicity of small tank-fights, seeking to wear down the enemy's strength by an attrition process based on their own growing superiority of numbers. They could afford to lose two or three tanks for one of the enemy if the attrition exhausted the Germans' scantier resources.

The tendency was accentuated both by the infantry's constant cry for tank support and by the tank crews' cry for bigger and bigger tank-guns. The less confidence these had in their own skill of manoeuvre, the more they clamoured for a decisively powerful gun, as well as thicker armour. So the tank itself grew bigger and heavier, while dwindling in manoeuvrable number. The compound effect of these factors was that, in the later stages of the war, tank-battles

193

declined into gun-duels between the individual tanks or small units. The few exceptions to the rule occurred when the German tank-strength was temporarily reduced to a shadow —as it was on the eve of the Allied break-out from Normandy. But most of the later battles were serial slogging matches, in which quickness of shooting by the individual tanks counted for much more than the quickness of formation manoeuvre. It was warfare with tanks, rather than tank warfare.

From this survey of the past we come to the future. The basic lessons have continuing value, but are too often forgotten.

The development of thermo-nuclear weapons has gone far to annul the prospects of success in all-out war, because that kind of war is so likely to result in mutual annihilation. So the likelihood of another great war has greatly diminished. But the possibilities of limited war have not diminished to the same extent, and have even been increased.

Although internal outbreaks call mainly for infantry, to restrict and suppress them, mobile armoured troops can do much both to damp and disperse them. In meeting more direct aggression, they form the most effective answer to a sudden pounce. Moreover, if such limited aggression should spread, and develop into nuclear war, an armoured force has a much better chance of survival, and of movement, than infantry.

Armoured forces, however, need to be remodelled on a more flexible and less vulnerable pattern. That is essential because the threat of nuclear bombing or missile bombardment will be a constant shadow. It is also essential to avoid being disrupted, or paralysed, by non-nuclear air and missile attack. The Western forces will no longer enjoy their immense advantage in 1944–45 of moving under a vast air umbrella against an opponent who was almost devoid of such cover overhead. In manoeuvring against invading forces they must reckon with very serious interference from the air. Moreover, because of relatively greater supply needs, Western armies are more susceptible to paralysis than armies of Soviet type.

Since the Western Powers are faced by opposing armies of greatly superior size, their chance of successful resistance vitally depends on being so mobile, both strategically and tactically, that they can outmanoeuvre the attacker. It is not only a matter of the small armoured units having the utmost possible battlefield agility, so that they can shift quickly from one fire-position to another, but of divisions being able to switch rapidly from one sector to another to deliver deep in-and-out counterstrokes, with the aim of hamstringing the invader.

That calls for a new kind of organisation. The armoured divisions that proved so decisive in 1940 had gone less than half-way towards fulfilling the design I had visualised in 1920. Every vehicle in an armoured force ought to have cross-country mobility, and at least sufficient protective armour to keep out bullets and shell-splinters. The present-type armoured force is gravely lacking in manoeuvring flexibility. Its long road-bound tail makes it almost as rigid as the shaft of a spear. We ought to develop it into a mechanical snake.

Besides giving the tail flexibility, this should be reduced in size. The most potent effect of an armoured stroke comes from the sudden concentration of tanks against a weak spot in the enemy's dispositions. But the armoured division of the last war became so bulky and long in the tail that even when coiled up close it was difficult to concentrate many tank-fangs in one sector, and even more difficult to concentrate them quickly. To make this practicable it is necessary to reduce the auxiliary components, thus increasing the ratio of the tanks to the formation as a whole.

Tactical

The tactical idea which inspired the creation of armoured forces was that of *fighting mounted*—to gain mobility and maintain momentum—as the cavalry did in the times when they were the decisive instrument of battle. The incorporation of men who can fight on foot is a tactical necessity—for ferreting out enemy troops who are under cover behind obstacles, and for various defensive tasks. But it is a basic error of organisation if the proportion of infantry exceeds the proportion that fights mounted, manning armoured fighting vehicles and self-propelled guns. Armoured fighting men ought to be preponderant in an armoured force if it is to justify its name and fulfil its purpose.

Moreover, for tactical efficiency, the mounted infantry element of the force needs to have a cross-country mobility closely equivalent to that of the armoured fighting element. This condition can only be met if the whole of the infantry element is carried in armoured personnel carriers. Otherwise it will not be able to accompany the tanks closely enough for prompt action to clear defended obstacles which block the tanks. There is abundant experience to show that the quicker these foot-fighters can intervene, the fewer will be needed. A company of armoured infantry coming into action immediately they are needed, might brush away resistance that a whole battalion of ordinary motorised infantry, brought up later, could not overcome when the obstacle has been reinforced. Time is decisive in war, and even more in quenching a local threat before it spreads into a general conflagration.

There must also be a drastic reduction in supply requirements, and vehicles, in order to attain adequate mobility. To that end, armoured troops ought to apply the principle that Sherman practised a century ago, and by which he revived mobility in the later stages of the Civil War, prior to his advance through Georgia and the Carolinas. Modern

196

mobile forces must likewise learn how to " slim "—to reduce their military " fat " in order to increase their mobility and endurance. They ought to be capable of operating self-contained for several days, or even weeks, instead of being tied to vulnerable lines of supply. Moreover, supply by air needs to be employed to the fullest practicable extent—and this should become more fully possible as the helicopter is improved, or superseded by new ground-hopping vehicles. That would also enable a reduction of the foot-fighting and other auxiliary elements.

While much can be gained by organisational progress, it is no less important to achieve a new advance in tank design. A fresh trend is already developing. Successive efforts to mount a bigger gun and thicker armour trebled the weight of tanks in the course of the last war—at the expense of tactical agility and strategic mobility. The heavier types of tank became, and remain, a serious handicap to speed and flexibility to manoeuvre, strategic and tactical.

The tank of the future will need to be fitted with night-driving vision, and with radar if possible. It should also be able to pass safely over a radioactive stretch of ground. If such requirements were to be combined with a heavy gun and heavy over-all armour, the tank would become an increasingly clumsy monster. The development of the guided missile is likely to cut short the reign of such monsters, while providing a substitute for their role.

So our primary objective should be a lighter tank of greater power; to make the tank lighter through the development of a new and lighter kind of hard hitting weapon. Also, by an effective solution of the problem of mounting the main weapon externally instead of in the turret. Thirdly, by lighter weight protection to replace the present armour plate. Fourthly, by a new form of motive power. We must always be seeking a technical break-through—to achieve a

revolutionary change. Meanwhile, we should strive to reconcile an effective gun-armour combination with manoeuvrability, keeping constantly in mind the guiding principle
" smaller and better ".

Our goal in tank specification and design should be to
produce a mechanised David instead of a Goliath. We
should aim to get a thoroughly effective battle tank that is
capable of being carried by air. That means a weight, under
present conditions, of not more than twenty-two or twenty-
three tons. Moreover, thirty to forty tons is about the
maximum for effective logistical properties under any physical
conditions we can visualise.

There is need of a fresh effort to develop a lighter and
cheaper type of tank. It must have adequate cross-country
capacity, which requires length of chassis, but not necessarily
bulk or weight in proportion. There is much to be said for
the combination of a swarm of highly mobile and relatively
light tanks with a hard core of heavy tanks. The right balance
between *numbers* and *power* (concentrated in a single machine)
is not easy to reach. But in history the tactics of the Mongol
armies, and also of the Byzantines at their best, tended to
show that a combination was superior to relying on one or
other factor alone. Another new possibility is to develop
remote-control tanks for the spearhead. With such un-
manned tanks there would be no deterrent moral effect from
heavy losses in applying saturation tactics—swamping the
opponent by confronting him with more separate assailants
than he can cope with.

Beyond the importance of lighter tanks, there are also
other lines of development towards greater mobility and
flexibility. One of these is the development of new kinds of
obstacle clearing equipment; another, new kinds of tank
bridging equipment—or, better still, new flotation devices to
make any tank capable of swimming rivers without having to

pause more than briefly for adjustment, and without diminution of its fighting efficiency.

It is also very important to develop helicopters or other new forms of direct lift aircraft for supply, except in first line transport. In this first-line transport we need vehicles with greater cross-country capabilities. A still greater advantage is promised through the prospect of air flotation—by the fuller development of zero ground pressure vehicles, capable of short grasshopper-like jumps over obstacles, or of more lengthy tactical hops to the scene of action on the ground.

A further need, particularly for an army that has to deal with oversea emergencies, is for an adequate scale of tank landing ships. It becomes more essential, for an oceanic Power, as the prospect of strategic air movement is becoming restricted by the increasing unwillingness of continental countries, especially in Asia and Africa, to allow it to use bases on their territory, or even fly over it.

Changing conditions also call for changes in tactics. The offensive and counter-offensive success of armoured forces in World War II was dangerously dependent on freedom from air interference. The principle of concentration must be interpreted and applied in a new and more fluid way, with the aid of a new technique of controlled dispersion.

Now that the development of nuclear weapons has led to a situation of nuclear stalemate—only breakable through mutual suicide—the traditional aim of destroying the enemy's main armed forces has become obsolete, and utterly absurd. For to pursue such an absolute aim is the surest way to induce on the opposing side a feeling of desperation that will produce mutually fatal results. Strategically and tactically, the only sensible aim now is, not the destruction, but the *paralysation* of the enemy's action. In pursuing this aim the capture or maintenance of positions will count for much less than the domination of areas—which is best achieved by offensive (and counter-offensive) fluidity of force. Such fluidity of force is a principle that fits the future, because it is adapted to the new conditions, and mobile armoured forces are particularly well fitted to fulfil it.

19

THE DEVELOPMENT OF NIGHT ACTION

A CLOAK of invisibility is the best means of surprise, and better than any armour as a means of protection. Moreover, the cloak that Nature provides nightly has the advantage of being more consistent and predictable than any artificial one. Its value, however, depends on the degree of training far more than in the case of other tactical aids. Darkness is a friend to the skilled soldier, but a cause of confusion to the unskilled.

The greatest handicap has always been that of soon forgetting lessons learned, and of repeatedly slipping back after any step forward. It may thus be useful, and not merely of historical interest, to provide an account of the efforts made between the wars, and of their effects.

Night attacks were very rare in World War I. The general reluctance to try such a course was all the more curious since the machine-gun dominated the battlefield and was the main factor in producing the prolonged deadlock, while losing much of its deadliness in conditions of poor visibility. Yet although the difficulty of assaulting a well-entrenched enemy in daylight was universally recognised, the possibilities of assaulting under cover of darkness were neglected, except in minor attacks and raids. Commanders were so obsessed with the risks of confusion that they habitually chose the more certain risks of annihilation for their troops and stultification for their plans.

One of the few exceptions to this rule of abstinence was

the attack delivered by the British Fourth Army in the second phase of the Somme offensive, on July 14, 1916.

In the opening phase on July 1 excessive reliance had been placed on the paralysing effect of the seven-day bombardment—from 1,500 guns concentrated on a fourteen-mile front—and the infantry assault was launched in full daylight, at 7.30 a.m. to ensure good observation for the artillery. The army commander, Rawlinson, privately felt some doubts but, as the Official History itself records, he " impressed on all at conferences and other times that ' nothing could exist at the conclusion of the bombardment in the area covered by it ' and the infantry would only have to walk over and take possession ". The outcome was a loss of 60,000 men for a very small gain of ground—only on the right wing, and less than a mile at the deepest. It was the heaviest day's loss in the whole history of the British Army.

During the next two weeks a series of nibbling attacks brought the British right wing gradually closer to the German second line, about two miles behind the original front. Meanwhile, the Germans were deepening the fortified belt faster than the British could nibble into it, so that if the British waited until they were near enough the second line for close assault they were likely to be faced with a barrier as strong as on July 1. But in trying to hasten the delivery of his next big blow, aimed to break through the second line on a four-mile sector between Delville Wood and Bazentin-le-Petit, Rawlinson had to reckon with the awkward fact that his right-hand corps was still three quarters of a mile distant from the enemy's second line. The solution he chose was that the troops should cross the exposed area in moonlight and storm the German line at 3.25 a.m.—before the sunlight was clear enough for the defending machine-gunners to see their targets. The assault was to be preceded by a hurricane bombardment of only five minutes' duration.

The Development of Night Action

In 1916 the idea of such a night advance and the idea of such a brief bombardment were both so fresh in revival as to shock orthodox opinion and appear a gamble. The Commander-in-Chief, Haig, was very dubious about the plan, but eventually let Rawlinson have his way. The results were strikingly successful, and a complete break-through could have been achieved if the exploitation had matched the initial thrust. The cavalry came up in the evening to make their first appearance on the battlefield since 1914, but merely showed the futility of horse-mounted troops as an instrument of exploitation in the machine-gun age.

The cost of the break-in of July 14 was extraordinarily small compared with that on July 1. Yet the enemy trenches were but slightly damaged on the second occasion whereas they had almost been obliterated on the first—the enemy machine-gunners then having moved out into the multitudinous shell-holes, which provided them with all too effective alternative fire-positions. One of my own most vivid memories from then on was the contrast between the battlefield on July 1, with thick swathes of khaki-clad corpses far outnumbering those in field-grey, and the battlefield on July 14 when the proportions were manifestly the reverse. The impact of that 1916 impression had a lasting effect on my tactical thinking. When given the opportunity to write the post-war *Infantry Training* manual, I emphasised the value of night action, of smoke, and of surprise in every form. But the prescriptions in the draft were watered down by the War Office before the new manual was finally issued.

Among the points I emphasised at this time was that: " The cloak of darkness has the advantage over smoke in that it enables surprise in *time*—whereas smoke warns the enemy—as well as in direction and concentration. While surprise is the principal purpose in operating at night, this also gains security in two ways—security to plans from air observation; security to personnel from air bombing and machine-gun fire."

Ten years later, in the course of writing my history of the war, I was struck by the frequency with which there had been foggy conditions at the start of a number of the more successful offensives. This observation prompted me to make an analysis of all the offensives launched on the Western Front during the war, and it became evident that fog—which provided a cloak of obscurity for the assaulting troops—had prevailed on almost every occasion when a deep and rapid penetration was achieved. One found that fog cloaked the French attack close to the Somme on the morning of July 1, 1916. Fog cloaked the remarkably successful French offensives that autumn, which regained in two quick bites most of the ground lost during the prolonged German offensive from February to July. Fog cloaked the great surprise stroke at Cambrai in November 1917. Fog cloaked all the three breaks-through by the Germans in 1918, but was absent in their three abortive offensives of March 28, June 9, and July 15. It shrouded the battlefield for the benefit of the British on the morning of August 8, 1918, and came to the aid of the 46th Division when it broke the Hindenburg Line on September 28. These were only some of the most striking examples.

Reflection on these facts suggested that, as the planners of an offensive cannot always reckon on there being a natural fog—especially in summer, when other conditions are most favourable for an offensive—a greater effort should be made to develop alternative possibilities of cloaking the assault. One was to produce artificial fog, by finding a means of developing the smoke screen on a much bigger scale. The other was to utilise darkness—this being a consistently calculable daily cloak of obscurity. After reaching these conclusions, I started a campaign to exploit the potentialities of both these methods. To diminish their handicaps I urged (*i*) a much more thorough system of training in night operations; (*ii*) scientific research into the possibilities of producing artificial moonlight, provided as and when required, particularly for exploiting the initial break-in.

My reasons for the latter proposal may be made clearer by reproducing here some passages from a lecture I gave to the officers of Southern Command in 1931 on " The Future of Infantry "—and later printed as a booklet—

Obscurity is the natural antidote to the machine-gun, and may prove a better antidote than armour in the long run.

Hence I would urge that the chemical service might profitably concentrate its efforts on the production of artificial fog. I use the term not as a synonym for, but in distinction to, the present smoke screen. This is helpful, but too local. I hope that we may explore the possibilities of covering a whole belt of country with fog. Its value is accentuated if we recognise that the true function of infantry is to disorganise the resistance, not merely to push it back.

For this reason, also, the revival of the night attack is due—overdue. Its moral ripples spread disorganisation far beyond the physical reach. And its risks, of confusion, are less than those of slaughter, from machine-guns with an unobscured field of fire. The former risks can be reduced by training, but even with hurriedly trained troops we have only to compare the results, and cost of the attack on July 1, 1916, with that on July 14, to see that a clear light for the enemy machine-guns is far the greater risk.

Is there any way to extend the physical reach of the night attack ? This is worth consideration, for unless we can there is a great danger of falling into a habit of launching attacks just before dawn in order that the exploitation may begin in daylight. Any regular habit is more dangerous in war, because more certain of finding the opponent ready, than the greatest of hazards that possesses the sovereign virtue of unexpectness.

Because light is so important for effective exploitation, I am led to speculate on the possibility of developing artificial light as well as artificial fog. In that case we might launch an attack to penetrate the enemy's position several hours before dawn, and assist the process of exploitation by flood-lighting the battlefield until daylight arrives. Whether that flood-lighting might be done by a co-ordinated series of powerful flares dropped from aircraft, by super-flares of great intensity and duration fired from the ground, or by mechanised searchlight groups, I do not presume to determine. That is a problem for light experts, not light infantry experts, to explore. But one can perceive that artificial light would have one priceless advantage over natural light—that of being controllable. If two antagonists are in a darkened room, the one who has his hand on the electric light switch has an incalculable advantage.

Soon afterwards a powerful reinforcement came from the publication, in January 1932, of the Official History of the Somme Battle. Its revelations about the opening assault came as a shock to the Chief of the Imperial General Staff, Field-Marshal Sir George Milne—who, from 1915 on, had been away from the Western Front, commanding in Macedonia. He appointed a War Office Committee (of eight generals, Sir Walter Kirke presiding) to investigate the lessons of the war, and whether they were being applied in the training manuals and training of the Army. Being consulted, and asked to prepare a paper on the subject, I had an opportunity of helping to get a number of conclusions adopted in the Committee's report—thanks particularly to Major-General (later Lieutenant-General Sir Bertie) Fisher. The primary conclusions were the need for surprise, and the means of achieving it; the development of night attacks; the conversion of a " break-in " into a " break-through " by an accelerated technique of exploitation—employing a completely mechanised force, supported by assault aircraft, and applying quickened means of intercommunication, fuller development of wireless, more forward command, and less elaborate orders. Other points were the need for developing the technique of, and training in, the counter-attack and counter-offensive; the lightening of the soldier's load; and the simplification of drill.

Two of the key passages in this Report were—

The Importance of Surprise
As a result of our study we are impressed with the paramount importance of surprise both in attack and defence.

206

The Development of Night Action

We consider that the greatest lesson to be gathered from the World War is that no attack in modern war is feasible or likely to succeed against an enemy in position unless his resisting power has already been paralysed either by:
- (a) some form of surprise; or
- (b) preponderating fire, powerful enough to produce the effect of surprise.

The conclusion is that movements by night may often be the only way of obtaining a tactical surprise, and attack by night the most economical way of crowning it by tactical victory.

It has been pointed out that many of the attacks on the Western front owed their success to fog and this for the same reason, viz. the blinding of the defenders' machine-gunners. The first battle of Gaza was probably lost because we did not take advantage of a similar opportunity.

We agree that the great importance of a cloak of obscurity, darkness, fog or artificial smoke should be stressed, and in our training more attention be paid to:
- (a) moving at night on wide frontages;
- (b) working in foggy weather;
- (c) the use of the compass.

In conclusion we are of opinion that our training manuals require to emphasise more strongly the vital importance of surprise and of the indirect approach, and we suggest that a sentence be added to Field Service Regulations, Vol. II, 1929, Sec 25(2), to the following effect:

A commander who selects the offensive and fails to surprise his opponent has lost the main advantage which the offensive confers.

Increased Importance of Night Operations

The main stumbling blocks in the way of the attackers are the defenders' machine-guns. Though it is obvious that one cannot defeat them by walking up to them, yet attack plans have at times failed to recognise this elementary truth. We can deal with these machine-guns in three ways:
- (1) Stalking them—this can only be done against weak, or ill-organised defence;
- (2) Damaging them—by shell, bullet, tank or gas;
- (3) Blinding them—by smoke, fog or night.

. . . attacks by night . . . it is doubtful whether they are sufficiently practised in peace training . . . night attacks are usually practised by a wrong method. They are made the climax of the operation. This is wrong. They should usually be the prelude to further operations. If his surprise has come off, and his night attack has become a success, the commander has only been successful in a " break-in " . . .

This Report was a big step forward. Yet in the sequel only a few commanders made a serious effort to apply its recommendations about training for night action. In Northern Command, the training instructions for 1933 drafted by Colonel (later Field-Marshal) H. R. Alexander took the Report as their keynote. In the Aldershot Command, Brigadier (later Field-Marshal) A. P. Wavell, commanding the experimental 6th Infantry Brigade, practised night operations intensively in his exercises. The most intensive development of all was in Egypt, by Brigadier (later General) Sir Frederick Pile, commanding the Canal Brigade. In planning the manoeuvre season it was decided " to fight entirely at night and sleep by day ". At first the troops were apt to get lost, so during the non-manoeuvre season they were made to go out for an hour or so every night into the desert and find their way about.

Speaking of this period (1933-34) in his memoirs, and of the general outlook prevailing beforehand, Pile says—

It was considered that an attack carried out by a company was possible, but that attacks on a much larger scale had in history generally led to disaster. I believed that the reason such attacks had failed was that the troops had not been adequately trained for night work, and that with such training it should be possible to maintain direction just as easily by night as by day, with the added advantage that the number of casualties would be very greatly reduced. I had very strong support from Jock Burnett-Stuart, who encouraged me to try everything, and in particular never to call a halt to an exercise at night however muddled the troops became, but to continue right through to dawn and see what transpired then.

I have found in my files a copy he sent me of some training instructions he issued—characteristically pungent. They contain so much basic guidance which remains just as applicable today, a quarter of a century later, that it is well worth quoting them at some length—

We still regard a night operation as a very hazardous and uncertain thing. We are frightened of losing ourselves; we are frightened of the confusion that will arise, and we are not prepared to chance it unless all the circumstances are favourable. The fact is we have not put our whole hearts into this training for night operations; and yet the most difficult thing for an enemy to compete with is a night attack. Every advantage is on the side of the attacker.

There are certain principles. The troops must be well and continually exercised in working in the dark. There must be no fear that anybody will lose their way. In this country, with the stars to guide us, it is ridiculous to halt every ten minutes or so to check compass bearings. Continual halts in a night march are very tiring and bad for the troops. Having got into the enemy's position, we must have a lot of men on the ground, and here lies the big difference between a daylight and a night attack. The reserve in the hands of the Commander ready to clear up any situation, and with its liaison officers forward, must always be available. Commanders must allot *area* objectives to assaulting troops so that they can be certain that that particular area in the objective will be cleared of the enemy and held. Commanders themselves must be well up in the battle. Of course, as in all attacks, the simpler the plan the better, but that does not mean that one should go forward like a sledgehammer. A well trained Brigade should be capable of doing a flank march at night over unknown ground and carrying out an attack during the hours of darkness and arriving at its objective.

The Technique—and by that I mean the complete " drill "—of night attacks can and should be perfected so that it is unnecessary before a night operation to issue any order other than that for the particular operation in view.

The approach march up to the time contact has been gained with the enemy is, generally speaking, a daylight affair. This phase gives great opportunities for practising all the drill of attack, and it is during this phase, as pointed out by the G.O.C., that it is the first duty of the advance troops to locate enemy machine guns. When, however, the enemy's advance elements have been pushed back and we are up against his main position, the attack must either be supported by a large number of other arms or else must take place in the dark.

During this Training Season, *all* such attacks will be carried out as night operations, and will be carried right through till dawn. Efforts will be made to mix up companies and platoons, and so to practice the reorganisation from the confusion which might result from a night

209

attack. Reorganisation from this confusion can well be practised by Companies during daylight, and this should be the first step. Company Commanders can run a short scheme disorganising their Company and placing their sections and platoons in doubtful tactical situations, such as they might have reached on the conclusion of a night attack, and then, at a certain moment, letting platoon and section leaders re-organise their commands.

In every platoon there are certain men better adapted than others to guide their units at night. These men must be encouraged and trained so that their special abilities may be available for their units. Head-quarters from Battalions downwards should each have specialists cap-able of guiding their unit and ready at a moment's notice to tell their Commander exactly where they are.

During Brigade Training, I propose directing all our energies to per-fecting this night work, and I hope by the time we go to HELWAN that it will be impossible for any unit, however small, to lose itself in the dark; and that the disorganisation bogey will once and for all have been laid by a continual practice in readjusting our positions and re-organising our units after they have been engaged in a night attack.

The results of these efforts are not hard to trace. The Canal Brigade at that time contained an extraordinary num-ber of soldiers who made their mark in the next war. One of them was Lieutenant-Colonel (later Field-Marshal) Mont-gomery, who commanded the 1st Royal Warwickshires.

Montgomery, at first sceptical about night action, became an ardent convert. Describing the change, Pile says in his memoirs—

Monty, who had been at one time opposed to night tactics on a large scale, brought off on one exercise a seven-mile approach march in the dark, followed by an attack with the whole of his battalion against a battalion of Guards, which he surprised and put completely in the bag. I often wonder whether when he was planning the great Battle of El Alamein that bloodless triumph remained in his mind.

That question is answered in Alan Moorehead's biography of him:

As for Montgomery himself, he was learning fast. There was one not-able exercise against a rival force which was defending the Pyramids. Up to this point Montgomery had been a little chary of night actions ; they were untidy, the formations were apt to get out of touch. But now it was essential if he was going to eliminate the enemy that they should be surprised. De Guingand, his old student from York, had now joined him, and the two men planned this, their first mock battle in the desert, together. . . . His men rushed upon the rival encampment in the darkness, and under the light of flares dropped from the air they mopped up the whole position.

It is hardly likely that either Montgomery or de Guingand could have felt the touch of history at that moment. Yet before ten years were out the things they learned on this night were going to engulf a million men in one of the decisive struggles of the world ; and all this was to happen in much the same way and not fifty miles from that same valley of the desert.

For on returning to Egypt in 1942 to take over command of the Eighth Army, Montgomery exploited night action repeatedly as his key method of breaking into the enemy's defences. The opening assault at Alamein, on October 23, 1942, was launched an hour after midnight. The further thrusts were mostly made under the cloak of darkness—and Rommel says in his *Papers*: " Night attacks continued to be a particular speciality of the British." That was demonstrated again when breaking into the Mareth line, the Wadi Akarit line, the Enfidaville line, and the enemy's final line covering Tunis—May 1943.

The development of artificial moonlight as an aid to night action was more tardy, and it did not come into use until the invasion of Normandy in 1944. But it played an important part in the later stages of the war. Montgomery paid high tribute to its value in his final dispatch: " The tendency to do more and more by night has been greatly facilitated by the provision of ' artificial moonlight '."

After so much proof, and such striking proof, of what night action can achieve, it is depressing that another slip back has occurred during the last decade.

The slip-back has also extended to night action by armoured forces—the potentialities of which were strikingly demonstrated as far back as 1926 in Aldershot Command manoeuvres. Much was done to develop it by Hobart with the first Tank Brigade in 1934–36—where practice produced such a pitch of skill that cross-country operations in the dark became nearly as fast as in daylight—and later with the Mobile Division in Egypt (which became the 7th Armoured). Caunter was another enthusiast who contributed a lot to this development when commanding the 1st Royal Tanks in Egypt and then when he took command of the 4th Armoured Brigade in the autumn of 1939. He also achieved much progress in night-firing technique.

These efforts paid a high dividend in the opening campaign in North Africa. Likewise in Crusader, a year later, much profit was derived from the intensive training in night action that had been practised in the 1st Army Tank Brigade, under Brigadier H. R. B. Watkins. The night break-through at Ed Duda on November 26, 1941, by the 44th Royal Tanks under Lieutenant-Colonel H. C. J. Yeo not only achieved the link-up with the besieged Tobruk garrison, but was largely decisive in causing Rommel to abandon his counterstroke. The night attack on Bardia on January 1, 1943, by the same troops, was decisive in producing the fall of that fortress.

But it becomes all too evident in examining the records of armoured operations in World War II that the standard and practice of night action began to slip during the war—as the original trained personnel became casualties. Moreover, there has been all too little sign of a revival since the war, either in the way of intensive training or in the development of technical aids.

A fresh step forward is overdue. In the last few years it has come to be recognised that the new conditions of warfare in the atomic era call for a far greater degree of dispersion than ever before, and much progress has been made towards developing a technique of controlled dispersion. But there is also urgent need of developing the skilled use of obscurity in every form.

Experience has shown that, in the dark, the more static arms like infantry and artillery have great difficulty in gauging the direction and speed of armoured troops, so that these have much to gain by exploiting the cloak of obscurity. The potentialities of night action on their part are increased by new means, particularly infra-red, a radiation " eye " which aids both movement and firing in the dark, while it does not reveal itself and cannot be jammed as radio waves can. Even so, the basic factor of success in operating at night is still that of superior training, which implies constant and abundant practice. In the dark the advantage of skilled over unskilled troops is doubled or trebled in comparison with action in daylight.

The need to revive and develop such training in the NATO forces is the more urgent because of growing evidence in recent years that the Soviet mechanised forces, particularly their spearhead divisions in East Germany, are being intensively trained in the combination of dispersion and night action. Indeed, it has become known subsequently that at times extensive manoeuvres have been in progress there for several days before it was realised, in the West, that such exercises were being carried out.

PART FIVE

ALTERNATIVE PROPOSALS

20

PASSIVE RESISTANCE

NEARLY ten years ago it was mutually agreed between the Governments that American air bases should be established in Britain and other countries on the eastern side of the Atlantic—as part of the atomic deterrent to a possible Russian attack. That momentous decision was accepted by the public with little question, producing only a few ripples of protest. Even after the first test explosions of an H-bomb in 1954 there was no corresponding growth of public anxiety. Nor at the end of that year, when the NATO Governments agreed in Paris that such strategic nuclear weapons should be reinforced with tactical nuclear weapons. Public and parliamentary awakening to the tremendous hazards of such means of protection was surprisingly slow—until the startling news of the Sputnik shook the Western peoples out of their slumbering acceptance of the nuclear arms race.

From that moment, public anxiety rapidly increased. It received fresh impetus from the double disclosure that the American bombers were now kept in such a state of super-alertness that one out of three could take off at fifteen minutes' notice, and that they actually carried the H-bombs on exercise flights. A third impetus came from the announcement that nuclear missile launching stations were about to be established at various places in England.

In 1958 a public campaign against the H-bomb developed, and spread like wildfire. Some of the best-known and most influential writers and thinkers of the age joined it, and put themselves at the head of it. A large proportion of the younger generation in the universities have thrown themselves ardently into the campaign. Only political and military ostriches who prefer to bury their heads in the sand can continue to ignore it.

Having striven to point out the suicidal character of atomic weapons since they were first produced, and the fallacy of relying on such weapons as a defence, I am naturally inclined to welcome a general awakening to the danger and the drawbacks of such an insurance policy. However emotional the anti-Bomb campaign may be, it is basically sound common sense.

It is apparent, however, that most of the leaders of the campaign are much clearer in their arguments and minds about the urgency of discarding the H-bomb than they are about what to rely upon in its place.

But Sir Stephen King-Hall is an exception, and he produced a definite prescription in his book *Defence in the Nuclear Age*. The first part of it is a most striking exposure of the fallacies in present defence thinking and the flaws in NATO defence policy. He goes on to urge that we must find a better basis of defence than that of trusting to the deterrent effect of weapons which, if put to use, would be suicidal—and genocidal.

To find such a better basis, he argues, we must break through the " thought-barrier " of habitual ideas about war and the ways of meeting aggression. His own " burst through the barrier " leads him to the conclusion that " violence " has " outlived its usefulness " as a means of defence. It is being superseded by, and should be replaced by, " political warfare "—action to influence minds, not to destroy bodies. From his own close observation and knowledge of that field in World War II, King-Hall is able to show how little it was understood. He wants to see it de-

veloped, and believes that such political-psychological operations should not only aim at " the protection of our ideas
against enemy ideas ", but should be inspired by the offensive
spirit—to drive home to the Communist peoples the advantages of our way of life and comparative freedom.

He contends that the best way to develop this psychological
offensive effectively is to discard the idea of nuclear retaliation, along with preparations for it—and that in any case it
is no way of defence, while very dubious as a deterrent.

This reflection leads him on to the conclusion that Britain
should take the initiative in abandoning nuclear weapons—
and do so " unilaterally ", on her own, if others will not
follow suit. Nor should she be willing to let the Americans
cover her in that way. " If we contracted out of the H-bomb
business we must contract out of all connections which are
associated with H-bombs and this means saying to the
Americans: ' Unless *you* abandon the H-bomb business the
Anglo-American Alliance in its military aspects is at an
end.' "

King-Hall also considers that it is impossible for the West
to build up conventional forces strong enough to withstand
the Russians, and thus pointless to maintain our existing
scale of forces. Tactical nuclear weapons should be scrapped,
since their use is " almost certain to see-saw upwards to the
largest nuclear weapons ". He declares his conviction " that
as between Britain occupied by the Russian army and a
Britain a smoking radioactive charnel-house the former is
the lesser of two great evils ".

While he considers such invasion to be *unlikely*, as being
contrary to the trend of Soviet policy, he faces the *possibility*
frankly. To meet it, he proposes a defence policy of non-
violent resistance, and his final chapter presents a detailed
plan for " The training of the Nation " in such forms of
resistance.

It is remarkable, and deeply significant, that a man so combative by temperament and heredity should become a leading advocate of non-violent resistance. Son and grandson of admirals, he himself had a distinguished naval carreer, and was a graduate of both the Naval and Army Staff Colleges. Moreover events have proved his foresight about the trend of warfare. His courage, too, has been proved in several fields—but never more so than by the way he has dared to take up the pacifists' argument and risk being decried as such.

While the practicability of his proposals can be questioned, his argument presents a challenge which deserves the fullest consideration—and cannot be ignored. Arguments for abjuring force have so clear a moral basis that, in a country where Christian or humane ethics prevail, they start with a moral advantage over arguments for defence by violent means. In principle, they claim the respect of all decent men, while their simplicity strengthens their appeal.

Their moral advantage and their appeal become all the stronger in a time when the main means of defence is a weapon of indiscriminate massacre, and one that may prove fatal to all mankind, including generations yet unborn.

Even on practical grounds there is a stronger case for non-violence than is generally realised. Its power has been demonstrated at various times, and it has achieved some notable successes. But its advocates are inclined to overlook the fact that its main successes have been obtained against opponents whose code of morality was fundamentally similar, and whose ruthlessness was thereby restrained. It is very doubtful whether non-violent resistance would have availed against a Tartar conqueror in the past, or against a Stalin in more recent times. The only impression it seems to have made on a Hitler was to excite his impulse to trample on what, to his mind, was contemptible weakness—although there is evidence that it did embarrass many of his generals, brought up in a better code, and baffled them more than the violent resistance movements in occupied countries.

But the practice of non-violent resistance against a Government, by members of a religious or political movement that is cohesive in spirit, is a different matter to its use by a nation in a conflict of States. To offer any good chance of success here, it not only requires a higher collective discipline and fortitude than any army has attained, but requires this level to be attained by the nation as a whole.

The effectiveness of an army can be maintained by strong leaders supported by an adequate nucleus of staunch and highly trained troops, since it is the well-aimed shots which mainly count. But the effectiveness of non-violent resistance is undermined if even a small proportion of the community play into the opponent's hand—through weakness, self-interest or pugnacity.

Such instincts tend to be much more prevalent in a nation than in a sectional, and spiritual, movement. Comparatively, an army is more dependent on its strongest elements, while an unarmed force is more dependent on its weakest elements.

In sum, an examination of the course that King-Hall has espoused leaves two main doubts about its practicability as a national policy. The first is whether the nation as a whole, or any likely Government, could be persuaded to embark on such a revolutionary experiment. The second is whether the policy could be effectively practised and fulfilled by a *nation* —since human instincts such as fear, anger, and selfishness could all too easily wreck its prospects.

But while examination brings out the underlying difficulties of the non-violent or pacifist solution, we are still left with the problem—which is both vital and urgent. War is lunacy in the H-bomb Age, and any form of defence likely to result in nuclear war is merely extravagant nonsense. We have been spending twenty times as much on defence year by year as we did in the middle years between World Wars I and II, without having even the moderate degree of security we enjoyed then. Yet we cannot multiply our military expenditure without becoming bankrupt. So it is essential to find some more hopeful way towards security—a way that will bring sense into a defence policy that at present naturally looks to the people like suicidal nonsense.

The first step is to realise that the H-bomb is mainly a deterrent to attack of its own kind, and not to all risks of armed conflict. On the other hand, the deterrent to any large-scale conventional invasion is the *probability* that it would soon bring on nuclear war—for in face of obviously mortal danger the defending side tends to use every available weapon. A calculating aggressor has no wish to be involved in mutual suicide, so a massive invasion is not likely.

A realisation of these basic factors would go far to simplify the West's defence problem, and bring it within manageable cost—indeed, less than we are spending today.

The present scale of the West's nuclear effort is in excess of need or sense. It was conceived under the old and out-of-date idea of winning a war. It has been continued in the hope of being able to nullify the Russians' nuclear threat by knocking out all their launching sites—a hope that is now merely a vain dream. For actual *deterrent* purposes the need could be met by simply having sufficient H-bombs and their means of delivery to make the Soviet leaders realise that their great cities are as vulnerable as ours.

The further question remains whether Britain should strive to stay in the nuclear race. As its nuclear power adds comparatively little to the deterrent already existing it is not a necessary contribution, and it is thus very dubious whether the effort really increases Britain's influence in the alliance, or her prestige. Any considerations of that kind ought to be

222

weighed against the much more important consideration that so long as Britain persists in maintaining nuclear weapons, for prestige, other countries will want to develop them for the same reason.

The more widely such development spreads the greater is likely to be the danger of catastrophe, through hot temper or accident. It would be wiser for Britain to discard nuclear weapons if, by doing so, she can secure a general agreement among the countries which do not yet have them in an effective form, to abstain from developing them.

21

NEUTRALITY

WHAT light does recent experience throw on the possibility, for a nation, of maintaining neutrality if war breaks out among the Great Powers ?

It is very commonly said that neutrality is an out-of-date idea, and the experience of World War II is cited as proof. The fate of Denmark and Norway, of Holland and Belgium, in 1940 manifestly tend to bear out such an assertion. Each of these small countries sought to keep out of the conflict, and endeavoured to maintain a strictly neutral attitude.

But Norway and Denmark were invaded by the Germans in April, 1940; Holland and Belgium were their victims in May.

The following month, when Hitler was still engaged in completing the conquest of France, the Russians moved into and occupied the three Baltic States—Lithuania, Latvia and Estonia. In 1941 the Germans invaded Yugoslavia and overran that country within a week. In 1944 Bulgaria was occupied by the Russians. Such a series of failures to preserve neutrality would appear to show that neutrality is an obsolete idea and hope.

On the other hand it is often forgotten that there were a number of notable exceptions. Sweden, Switzerland, and Spain kept out of the war from the beginning to the end. So did the Republic of Ireland, while Turkey did not enter the war until the last moment—a step which enabled her to claim a place in the United Nations under the time-limit laid down at the Yalta Conference of the Big Three.

The success of these countries in maintaining their neutrality so long was not due to geographical remoteness, for they were all precariously close to the strategic tracks along which the war moved.

Strategically, and economically, it would have been very convenient for Germany to have had free passage through Sweden to the Atlantic coast of Norway, and later a link with Finland.

It would have eased the German armies' path into France in 1940 if they could have outflanked the eastern end of the Maginot Line by a move through Switzerland.

It would have been still more advantageous to them, from 1940 onward, to have had a clear run through Spain to Gibraltar, so that they could block the western end of the Mediterranean to the Allies.

No less valuable to the Germans would have been the advantage of being able to pass through Turkey to strike at Britain's position in the Eastern Mediterranean, down to the Suez Canal, and at the backdoor to Russia's oilfields in the Caucasus.

The greatest advantage of all, for Germany, would have come from the occupation of Ireland. For Hitler could thereby have gained a stranglehold on the British arteries of supply, provided that he could maintain his grip—this was the crux of the matter.

Yet none of these likely, and expected, extensions occurred. So it is worth while to probe deeper into the cases, and situations, where the neutrality of the smaller countries was violated, in seeking to find a clue as to the reason why they suffered while others remained intact.

In the case of Norway, her Atlantic coast was of great strategic importance to Germany, both in tightening the submarine blockade of Britain and loosening the British blockade. It also covered the approach to Germany's flank, and to the Gallivare mines on which she depended for iron-ore. At the same time Norway's forces were weak, and had no experience of war. Denmark was a necessary stepping stone to the occupation of Norway. The Danish forces were very weak and without experience, while in addition the country was geographically indefensible.

Holland was in an equally exposed position, and her forces suffered the same handicaps. Moreover, the southern part of Holland formed the easiest approach to the Belgian frontier. And a passage through Belgian territory was the only way in which the Germans could outflank the heavily fortified stretch of the French frontier—unless they went through Switzerland. Thus each of these violations of neutral territory was related to another.

Passing on to the subsequent cases of violated neutrality, it is very obvious why Stalin considered it necessary to occupy the Baltic States. They formed an avenue of combined land and sea approach to Leningrad, which he hoped to block by occupying them.

On the other hand when Hitler decided to attack Russia he felt it necessary to safeguard his southern flank, in the Balkans. At first he hoped to secure it by a political arrangement with Yugoslavia, but when the acquiescent régime there was overthrown by an anti-German *coup d'état*, he decided to quench the potential menace to his Balkan flank by a quick conquest of Yugoslavia and Greece. His attack succeeded all the more easily because Yugoslavia, although its forces were numerically strong, was very short of modern equipment and also suffered from internal disunity.

As for the much later case of Bulgaria, the occupation of that country in the course of Russia's advance through the Balkans was a natural step in her strategic outflanking move, and also towards ensuring Russia's post-war predominance in that region.

226

Neutrality

What are the conclusions which emerge from such a detailed examination ? The first is that in every case the victims were so vulnerable that their conquest was easy. The second is that their conquest was of great importance to the attacker's success in pursuing his main strategic purpose.

In comparison, the countries which succeeded in preserving their neutrality were less accessible—thanks to sea or mountain barriers—while having relatively stronger forces of their own, or being better placed for external reinforcement. At the same time a passage through them did not appear so indispensable to the violator's purpose.

From such an analysis, a reasonable conclusion would be that neutrality remains *possible* where a country is capable of sufficient resistance as to make it look likely that the cost to the aggressor will exceed his profit. If he has a great deal to gain he will naturally be willing to risk more, but even in that respect there is a limit to what he can risk if he is engaged with another Great Power.

How will the attempt to follow a policy of neutrality be affected to the Atomic Age ? On balance, it seems likely that such a policy will become more feasible than in the past, and less hazardous relatively—indeed, less acutely dangerous than the situation of small nations which enter into the defence system of one or other of the great atomic-armed powers.

In most of the cases where the neutrality of small countries has been violated, the violation has occurred some time after the outbreak of war—when the Great Powers, after the first clash, have started manoeuvring to gain advantage over their opponents. The few exceptions to this rule have been when the big aggressor has considered it essential, to early success, to pass through the territory of some small neutral in his opening move. The diminished likelihood of long wars, in the Atomic Age, should help to increase the chances of preserving neutrality.

As to the hazards of neutrality, at the worst they could be no worse than the fate of any small country on which H-bombs were dropped. Moreover, small neutrals are much less likely to be taken as a target than those small countries which have entered into one of the Great Power combinations—particularly those small countries which stand in the front line, occupy key-points, and provide strategic air bases. Neutrality is not a heroic course, but for a small country it may prove the most sensible course, especially in the Atomic Age.

22

DISENGAGEMENT

THE idea of separating the two great opposed alliances in Europe by mutual withdrawal of their forces, and establishing a safety space between them, has been brought to the fore in the last few years. Such a " disengagement ", as it is called, has become a widely discussed solution for the present deadlock, which might all too easily result in an explosion fatal to both sides—and to the human race.

In October 1957 Poland's Foreign Minister, Mr. Adam Rapacki, proposed to the United Nations an agreed ban on the manufacture and maintenance of nuclear weapons in both East and West Germany, and the inclusion of his own country in this atom-free zone. (A year later, following Western criticism of his plan, he expanded it to cover " conventional forces " and their reduction in the zone.)

In the autumn of 1957, too, Mr. George Kennan, America's most prominent expert on Soviet Russia, put forward a wider proposal in his B.B.C. Reith Lectures. He said that the one " reasonably hopeful " course that he could see lay in " separating geographically the forces of the great nuclear powers "—by " a general withdrawal of American, British and Russian armed power from the heart of the Continent " while inducing the countries there to refrain from " building the defence establishments around the atomic weapon ".

These proposals were all the more significant because they were conceived about the same time but separately and independently, as well as from widely different angles. Their publication in rapid succession did more to focus attention on the problem than ever before.

But the broad idea, of disengagement, was mooted long ago, and has been repeatedly revived by leading men in different countries, especially in Britain, when seeking a solution for the dangers of the world situation.* In 1955, it was raised by Sir Anthony Eden at the Geneva Conference. Earlier still, as well as more recently, it was urged by Mr. Hugh Gaitskell, Mr. Aneurin Bevan, and Mr. Denis Healey from the Labour Party side. It was an important part of the plan proposed in 1954 by Marshal of the R.A.F. Sir John Slessor. Mr. Lester Pearson, Canada's most thoughtful and influential spokesman in world affairs, has been another notable advocate of the idea. Mr. Macmillan has shown an inclination towards it, and the final Communiqué on his Moscow talks with Mr. Kruschev in 1959 significantly said that they " agreed that further study could usefully be made of the possibilities of increasing security by some method of limitation of forces and weapons, both conventional and nuclear, in the agreed area of Europe, coupled with an appropriate system of inspection ".

Mr. Kruschev has often spoken favourably of the idea, and endorsed the Rapacki plan for creating a zone in Europe free from atomic weapons, urging that it should be one of the main points for consideration at a " summit " conference.

While it is unlikely that the Polish Foreign Minister would have put forward his proposal unless assured of Russian support for it, this does not mean that it was merely a Russian-inspired move, designed to gain a strategic advantage for Russia. For the Poles had ample reason of their own to initiate such a proposal. The lines of communication of the Russian armies in Eastern Germany pass through

* A very useful summary is provided in Captain Eugene Hinterhoff's book, *Disengagement*, 1959.

Poland. So Poland would almost certainly be the first country to suffer atomic destruction if the Russians were to advance into Western Germany. For, in countering the Russian advance, the NATO powers would have no such hesitation about " atomising " the road and rail centres of Poland—to paralyse the Russian communications—as they would have about wiping out the cities and towns of the country, Germany, which they were trying to protect.

The Polish Government very naturally realises that their country would be a primary target if war came in this way. That was enough to make their proposal genuine. It is also the best assurance that, if any such plan were to be accepted by the Western Powers, the Poles would do their utmost to ensure that it was fulfilled—and to curb any aggressive move westward by the Russians. There is nothing so damping to the aggressive spirit, particularly in a midway country, as the prospect of the homeland becoming an atomic battle-field or " beaten zone ".

Such a prospect makes for hesitation in accepting the presence of atomic weapons even for purely defensive pur-poses. Although it has become a general assumption in the NATO countries that they cannot be defended by conven-tional weapons—because of Russia's great numerical super-iority in conventional forces—the peoples of those countries have shown little desire for a direct nuclear reinforcement. The Germans have been markedly reluctant to accept nuclear weapons as a *defence,* though they may be glad to have the distant support of American nuclear strength as a protective *deterrent.* The Norwegians and Danes are not even willing to have American bases on their soil lest these may become a target for atomic bombardment. So it is not surprising that the Poles should be anxious to become " atom-free ".

The Rapacki plan, while concerned primarily with atomic weapons, accorded quite well with the basic pattern of the

231

proposals which Eden put forward at Geneva in 1955. Eden there suggested the possibility of a mutual agreement to establish a zone of limited armaments, under inspection and control by both sides, with a completely demilitarised strip running through the middle of it. In that way the respective forces would be brought out of contact with one another, thus diminishing the risk of frontier clashes that could develop into a serious and spreading engagement.

What are the practical objections to the project of an atom-free zone ? Do they suffice to outweigh its benefits from a Western point of view ? The military objection most commonly expressed is that it would hinder the early use of atomic artillery and other short-range atomic weapons, leaving the forward troops without such support in meeting a Russian invasion. But now that the Russians have similar atomic weapons it is very dubious whether the defending forces on the Western side would profit in any way by initi-ating the use of such weapons. On balance, they might get more benefit from an atom-free zone. This would be a hind-rance to an attacker in bringing forward his shorter-range atomic weapons, of more precision, to stun the defence by surprise. It would diminish the risk of atomic war starting accidentally on some false alarm. It would tend to relax the tension that arises from fear of surprise or the trigger-happy impulsiveness of some local commander.

A more serious practical objection is the difficulty of defin-ing the meaning and conditions of " a zone free from atomic weapons ". Any such weapons have a two-piece composition —the projectile or bomb, and its means of delivery. If the restriction were applied only to the projectile or bomb, we should have to reckon with the awkward fact that such " ammunition " might too easily be hidden or stealthily brought forward. If the restriction were extended to the means of delivery, it would be more possible to keep watch and check on these, but more difficult to pick out for banning those which are capable of delivering an atomic projective or bomb.

If an agreement were to be reached, about establishing an atom-free zone, and reinforced by an adequate system of inspection, it should be a good check on the entry and use of the bigger means of delivery—such as long-range strategic missiles and bombers, which besides being very obvious in themselves require elaborate launching sites and large airfields.

But it is much more difficult to establish an effective check on the shorter-range atomic weapons. For all too much "progress" is being achieved in packing atomic explosive power into small containers, and in multiplying their explosive force relatively to size. Heavy artillery of normal calibre can already fire atomic shells, and aircraft of what can be broadly classed as fighter category can deliver atomic bombs. Such so-called tactical atomic weapons are powerful enough to destroy cities that are within their range, if the destruction of these cities serves the military purpose—offensively or defensively.

These awkward facts pointed to the need for a more extensive limitation than that offered by the original Rapacki plan. A much better insurance of peace and security could be provided by developing the plan to include a limitation of the size of the conventional forces maintained within the zone, and of their nominally conventional armament.

It would be better still if this interspace zone of limited armaments could be widened and lengthened in space—to increase the geographical separation between the nuclear-armed giants, the U.S.A. and the U.S.S.R. The closer they are in contact, the greater the risk of friction—and of such friction producing a fatal explosion in some accidental way, unintended by either side.

233

The whole world's security in the atomic age might be greatly increased by creating what has been called a neutral belt. It would be better described as an international safety belt—and more fully defined as a strategic interspace, between the great nuclear Powers, filled by countries which by common agreement would limit the size and arms of their forces, and would not be in military alliance with the nuclear Powers on either side.

No matter where their particular sympathies lay, the most vital interest of all the belt countries would be to keep clear of such military attachment—in order to keep clear of atomic destruction. It would be of no less vital interest to the great Powers to respect the detached position of the belt countries, since this would constitute the best guarantee of their own safety.

Such a safety belt might well be extended much further than has been visualised hitherto. Why confine it to West Germany, East Germany and Poland ? Many other countries might be glad to come into it eventually, and the extension would be valuable.

It is possible to visualise a Trans-Eurasian safety belt that would stretch from Spitzbergen to the Himalayas—embracing the four Scandinavian countries (Norway, Finland, Sweden, Denmark); the six central European countries (Germany, Poland, Czechoslovakia, Austria, Hungary, Switzerland); the five Balkan countries (Yugoslavia, Rumania, Albania, Bulgaria, Greece); Turkey and the Middle East countries; Persia, Afghanistan, Pakistan, India. The belt might be extended eastward to embrace Burma, Thailand and Indo-China—and then to Japan and Korea. In the West the three Benelux countries, and others, might choose to join it.

There would be many advantages, and few if any disadvantages, in the creation of such an extensive *interspace*—

of comfortable width compared with the present " fire curtain " along the Iron Curtain—between the rival giants with
their hair-trigger weapons.

It would also be the most hopeful way, perhaps the only
hopeful way, of securing the relaxation of Soviet Russia's
grip of her satellites, and a much less dangerous way than
that of fomenting or aiding insurrections.

It has long been recognised that the best way to check the
spread of a forest-fire, or minimise the risks of an explosion,
is to create an interspace. We should be wise to apply that
lesson of experience in the international sphere without
delay. Time presses in the Atomic Age.

23

AN INTERNATIONAL FORCE

PROPOSALS for creating an International Force as a help to the preservation of peace have been put forward many times, particularly after World War I. At the Disarmament Conference in 1932 the French proposed the creation of a powerful International Police Force armed with a fleet of bombers to enforce world order. Under their plan the larger types of bombers, artillery and tanks were to be handed over to this force.

Their insistent preference for this very large and devastatingly disciplinary kind of international force unfortunately delayed the adoption of the qualitative disarmament plan, on which all the other Great Powers had quickly agreed, and by which there would have been an effective abolition of all the heavier weapons that could destroy fortified frontier defences and cities. The argument which then developed went on until, a year later, Hitler gained power in Germany—and the prospect of disarmament withered.

After World War II, another grandiose project for an International Force was tabled. In 1945 the victors jointly agreed at the San Francisco Conference that the United Nations should be provided with its own armed forces—to " put teeth " into its Charter. In 1947 the Military Staff Committee produced a report laying down the principles on which this international force should be organised. The report comprised forty-one articles, and the members of the Military Staff Committee succeeded in agreeing on a large proportion.

Unfortunately they agreed that the force should be composed of separate national contingents instead of being an integrated force directly enlisted for the service of the United Nations. That decision became an increasing hindrance, as divergence of policy increased, to the formation of any force.

Thereafter the idea lapsed until it was suddenly revived, on a more moderate scale, in the Suez crisis of 1956. The General Assembly on November 4 passed a resolution, proposed by Canada, asking the Secretary-General to prepare a plan for setting up an " emergency international United Nations force to secure and supervise the cessation of hostilities " in Egypt. The plan was approved and the force formed with astounding speed—from contingents provided by a number of the smaller nations not directly concerned in the dispute. In barely ten days, on November 15, the first United Nations troops landed at Port Said, and moved to the frontier area in Sinai. Their strength was subsequently raised to a total of six thousand men. By general recognition this United Nations Emergency Force has proved of much value for its specific purpose.

In 1958, however, a different treatment was applied, of older kind, to another emergency which arose in the Middle East—the civil war in Lebanon. Although in itself a puny and squib-like affair, it was another grave reminder of the world's perils in the nuclear-weapon age—where even a mishandled squib might set off a catastrophic explosion. It also brought a fresh demonstration of the limitations of any big stick policy on the part of the Western Powers in present circumstances.

Their first reaction to the trouble in the Lebanon was on familiar and traditional lines. Mr. John Foster Dulles, the American Secretary of State, publicly declared that if the Lebanese Government requested military aid to deal with the insurrection, and check interference by Nasser, " we would

237

be inclined to go along with that ". The American Sixth Fleet was alerted, moved to the scene, and reinforced ready for intervention. The British Government flew paratroop reinforcements out to Cyprus that were obviously being placed close at hand for the same purpose.

But the shadow of armed intervention by the Western Powers carried with it that of counter-intervention by Soviet Russia, foreshadowing the grim possibility of a big blow-up. Realisation of that risk worked as a two-way check. Alarm and anxiety spread in the capitals of the world, making for hesitation even in the quarters that had favoured strong action. Very soon Mr. Dulles was talking of American intervention only as a last resort, and expressing belief that the " best way " to deal with such problems was through the United Nations.

Meanwhile the Lebanese Government's appeal for a United Nations emergency force to cover and seal its 200-mile long Syrian frontier, against infiltration from Nasser's United Arab Republic, had met with no more response than the despatch of a 100-man team of U.N. observers. No adequate force for the purpose could be quickly improvised except by utilising American and British contingents. But such a course was naturally regarded in other quarters as a barely disguised form of intervention for the preservation of Anglo-American interests and influence in the Middle East.

Fortunately, the immediate crisis was relaxed by the dual effect of a compromise and a diversion. The compromise was the agreed replacement of President Chamoun's Government in Lebanon by one more acceptable to the people of that country. The diversion came from the overthrow of the Government of Iraq by a military revolt, which looked menacing to the security of Iraq's neighbours. This prompted an emergency appeal from the Governments of Lebanon and Jordan for American and British help respectively, while the

238

appeal provided a justification for responding—three United States Marine battalions were landed in Lebanon next day, being subsequently reinforced by Army airborne troops, and British paratroops were sent to Jordan. This prompt action was successful, while the crisis soon subsided. Nevertheless the helpers found themselves in a very tricky and embarrassing situation, even though their conduct was very careful, and cautious.

Such situations are all too likely to recur—not only in the Middle East but in other parts of the world. Is there a better way in which such emergencies, so perilous to the world in this atomic age, can be met without the risks that now cause hesitation and delay ?

This clouded prospect raises afresh, and more urgently, the question of creating a permanent " international force " as a safeguard. Even on the small scale of the United Nations Emergency Force that was sent to Sinai, after the Suez clash, it could be of great value—and all the more because, being permanent, it would be available at the start of an emergency. Its prime value would not be as a fighting force but as a fire guard placed between countries that were at loggerheads. It could be called in on the appeal of either, and posted on the frontier ; the other would be far more reluctant to interfere with such a truly international body than to attack the forces of its hated neighbours.

If directly recruited by the United Nations Organisation it would be easier to provide a rather larger and speedier force than UNEF. For the United Nations' present dependence on national contingents has tended to rule out any contribution of troops from the nations closely interested in the dispute, or suspected of favouring one side or the other. Moreover, a fire guard force of moderate size (say 20,000 altogether including reserves) would involve fewer complications, military or political, and have a better chance of acceptance than the big kind of international fighting force—comprising an army, a navy and an air force—that has been visualised in the past.

While the national contingent basis may seem to be the simplest, it has proved to be the most difficult politically, and also militarily—for it is a multiplication of the problem of past allied forces.

There have been numerous cases in the past of different national contingents operating together, but their effectiveness has tended to vary with the number participating. While forces of two nations have often co-operated with fair success, the difficulty has always grown with an increase in the numbers. The successive alliances formed to resist Louis XIV's and Napoleon's domination repeatedly wrangled and broke down. In World War I there was constant friction, especially in the Macedonian campaign when six national contingents combined—French, British, Italian, Serbs, Russians and Greeks.

No quite comparable situation arose in World War II. For the other national contingents taking part in the later campaigns were all small compared with the British and American, and were dependent on supplies from the two bigger allies. Even these two had many sharp disagreements on policy and plans—as to when and where their combined forces would be used. In 1942 the Americans urged an early landing in France ; the British considered this futile, and fatal ; and the Americans threatened to shift their weight to the Pacific before a compromise was reached to land in French North Africa. In 1943 there was fresh dispute whether to push on through Italy or into the Balkans, and then about continuing through Southern France or Austria. Even after the success of the Normandy landing in 1944, further disagreement developed about the line of advance into Germany, and in 1945 over the question of thrusting to Berlin.

Closeness of contact too often accentuates divergences.

240

That is another lesson of experience between allies—similarly to what so often happens when grown-up members of a family live together under the same roof. Cross purposes and mutual criticism have been prevalent whenever forces of different nations have fought alongside one another. They tend to blame their allies for any reverse suffered and to claim for themselves most of the credit for any success gained.

Blucher and Wellington co-operated wonderfully well in the final defeat of Napoleon at Waterloo, but British histories of the battle barely mentioned Blucher's part, while Prussian histories conveyed that Wellington was only saved from disaster by Blucher's arrival. As soon as Napoleon was overthrown, and long before the histories were written, the allies were in discord about policy—and the British even thought of allying themselves with France against their former allies. In World War I Haig's diary was bitterly critical of the French, while the French commanders were no less acid about the British. In World War II the French, British and Belgians blamed one another for the common defeat in 1940, while British and American leaders are still hotly arguing about their respective shares in the final victory.

Any large and representative U.N. force would comprise more national contingents, on an equal basis, than in any of these cases of inter-allied operations. The nearest parallel was the international army formed to deal with the common threat to European interests of the Boxer Rebellion of 1900 in China. For it, eight nations furnished contingents. The common purpose was soon forgotten, and each nation tended to use its contingent to gain an advantage for its own interests in that part of the world.

If the scheme visualised by the United Nations in 1947 had been carried out, it would probably have repeated most of these faults of the past with some fresh ones added. The various national contingents were to retain their " national character ", including their distinctive systems of control and discipline. Each was to provide its own reinforcements, supplies and transport. That would certainly have led to competition and controversy over the respective use of ports, railways, and roads between so many equal partners, especially in any region where such facilities were scanty.

The weakest spot of any force is its administrative area—its supply system, bases, and lines of communication. This is where it is most liable to breakdown, and most vulnerable to interruption by the enemy. The weakness has increased with technical progress—the various types of weapon in any force now run to scores, its types of equipment to hundreds, and the component parts to thousands. That complexity, and weakness, would be vastly multiplied in any force composed of national contingents intent to maintain their " national character "—each requiring different rations to feed its men ; different calibres of ammunition to feed its weapons ; different spare parts and tools ; and each functioning on a different staff system.

A realisation of the difficulties that are bound to arise with a *national*-international force points to the advantages of the other form of such a force—composed of men directly enlisted for the permanent service of the United Nations. It could be organised and trained homogeneously. Its system of command, of communication and of supply would be uniform, together with its equipment and armament. It would be free from the fetters of national traditions, and could pick the best points of various patterns—as other recent " new armies ", particularly that of Israel, have done.

For convenience and clarity it would be best to adopt a single language for operational use. That has been done in many empires of the past, and would be less difficult now, as the personnel would be more intelligent and quicker to learn than those enlisted in the colonial forces of such empires.

English is the obvious choice, as it is now far more widely known and used than any other. In most armies today many of the officers can already speak it, particularly the younger ones.

The force should have its own motor transport, troopships and air transport. Arms and equipment for a force of such moderate scale present no major problem. Later, in an improved political atmosphere, the United Nations might take over the manufacture of major weapons. This would be the safest system.

The objection that an international force would lack the spirit which inspires a national army is much exaggerated. In most professional armies, national spirit has been a factor secondary to the soldierly spirit that grows from training, discipline, comradeship and a sense of mission. Napoleon's long-victorious army was a mixture of nationalities. So was Wellington's, which defeated it at Waterloo. A more recent example of the bravery and endurance that can be attained by a force composed of different nationalities is the French Foreign Legion. Mixed nationality should all the less affect an international force, because its members would not be fighting under the flag of one foreign nation.

Bases are a key problem. Concession of bases on national territory is not enough. They would be too exposed to interference. For security, a base needs a covering zone that cannot be easily dominated or penetrated. That need calls for the creation of international territories in different parts of the world—preferably island sites. One permanent base would suffice administratively. But for strategic handiness two would be desirable, and three better still—one in the Near East, one in the Far East, and one on the Atlantic side of Europe.

For the Near East, the most urgent case, Cyprus would be suitable geographically and strategically as a regional base.

Rhodes and Crete are alternative sites. In the Far East, one of the Philippine Islands might be the most suitable choice. There are several other possibilities. On the Atlantic side of Europe, the Swedish Islands of Gotland and Oland, the Danish island of Bornholm, and the Shetland or Orkney islands are some of the possible sites.

Once an international " fire guard " was established, and had produced a more stable situation, the way would be paved for its expansion into a larger and more strongly armed force capable of fulfilling a " peace-enforcement " role. This in turn would offer a possible solution of another fearful problem now looming on the horizon—the imminent spread of nuclear weapons among an increasing number of countries, and the consequent multiplication of the world's hazards. The best chance of curtailing this danger would lie in mutual agreement to hand over nuclear weapons to an international force. That would also much increase the chances of progress towards disarmament in general. It may look a dim hope today, but the increasing danger of mutual extinction should be a powerful incentive to try any alternative.

PART SIX
EPILOGUE

24

THE MOST HOPEFUL ROAD TO PEACE

THE Romans coined the maxim: " If you wish for peace, prepare for war." But the many wars they fought, and the endless series since their day, show that there was a fallacy in the argument—or that it was too simply put, without sufficient thought. As Calvin Coolidge caustically remarked, after World War I : " No nation ever had an army large enough to guarantee it against attack in time of peace or ensure it victory in time of war."

In studying how wars have broken out I was led to suggest, over twenty-five years ago, that a truer maxim would be : " If you wish for peace, understand war." That conclusion has been reinforced by World War II and its sequel. It signposts a *road* to peace that is more hopeful than buildingplans—which have so often proved " castles in the air ".

Any Plan for peace is apt to be not only futile but dangerous. Like most planning, unless of a mainly material kind, it breaks down through disregard of human nature. Worse still, the higher the hopes that are built on such a plan, the more likely that their collapse may precipitate war.

There is no panacea for peace that can be written out in a formula like a doctor's prescription. But one can set down a series of practical points—elementary principles drawn from the sum of human experience in all times. Study war, and learn from its history. Keep strong, if possible. In any case, keep cool. Have unlimited patience. Never corner an opponent, and always assist him to save his face. Put yourself in his shoes—so as to see things through his eyes. Avoid self-righteousness like the devil—nothing is so self-blinding. Cure yourself of two commonly fatal delusions—the idea of victory and the idea that war cannot be limited.

These points were all made, explicitly or implicitly, in the earliest known book on the problems of war and peace—Sun Tzu's, about 500 B.C. The many wars, mostly futile, that have occurred since then show how little the nations have learned from history. But the lesson has been more deeply engraved. And now, since the development of the H-bomb, the only hope of survival, for either side, rests on careful maintenance of these eight pillars of policy.

It may appear strange that the first point of advice for preserving peace should be to study war. But there is no better cure for an inclination to, and belief in, forcible solutions—provided that such study goes far enough.

But there is more beyond this to be learned from extending study of war and the evidence of history. It becomes clear that the surest way to prevent war is to avoid taking steps that, in experience, have precipitated it. Although this may be called a negative course, it is a form of negative that leads to positive benefit. For it keeps clear of courses that cause fatal accidents, while keeping the road open for the normal traffic between nations which promotes peaceful relations.

To limit the danger of war, unlimited patience is needed. That is not easy for the statesmen of the Western democracies, especially those who are by temperament eager for quick solutions. Even where the statesmen realise the necessity, they are under pressure from an emotional electorate. At the same time patience is extraordinarily strained in dealing with Eastern statesmen who are under no such pressure, and are accustomed to spinning out time. Yet as Sir Anthony Eden wisely remarked some six years ago, although he later appeared to forget the advice: "To jaw-jaw is always better than to war-war." The rising generation of statesmen should be trained to develop endless endurance in jaw-jaw. For the alternative, a show-down, can all too easily be suicidal in the H-bomb age.

On the other hand, the talk of a settlement is symptomatic of an outlook and attitude that puts expectations too high, even dangerously high. For nothing is so apt to create, or aggravate, a dangerous situation than the shock of sudden disillusionment. The people who most ardently expect and desire a peaceful settlement are the people most apt to suffer the worst reaction, even a bellicose reaction, when their hopes of a settlement are disappointed. Peace-planning too often seems to breed a sense of self-righteousness that provokes war, or precipitates it, instead of preventing it.

The word " settlement " has an unreal sense of finality in it —and thus paves the way for disillusionment. Study of history does not encourage much belief in its possibility, however desirable it may be. Politically, the settlements that Governments make are liable to be upset by changes of government, changes of popular mood, changes of friendship, changes of economic condition, changes in the balance of power. The kind of settlement that takes the form of a signed and sealed treaty is often the most precarious— because its fixity makes it less adjustable to changing conditions.

Nor does history make one hopeful about the possibility of arriving at a settlement about disarmament. There have been repeated attempts to make progress towards peace by this path, but no successes. While the pursuit of security in armament races has always proved fatal to peace, disarmament projects have never fulfilled their better inherent promise.

The proposal for a general scaling down of armaments seems the easiest solution, and has the most obvious appeal

—not least on economic grounds. But numerical scales form, in practice, the most difficult approach to the problem. When numbers come into calculation, it is hard to reach a general agreement about the scale that different countries deem requisite for their security. Each country is naturally inclined to exaggerate its own special circumstances, and over-estimate its own minimum needs—while failing to see the justification for what others claim. Thus a discussion of the relative *size* of national forces leads to interminable wrangling and to no definite conclusion.

Any such *quantitative* approach to the problem seems even more impracticable now. For Soviet Russia has such a large existing superiority in numbers, of men and machines, that any all-round reduction of a *proportionate* kind would do nothing to improve the security of the Western countries who are much weaker in armed numbers. It would entail the fixation of their present condition of inferiority. The effect could be dangerous psychologically as well as materially. A feeling of insecurity makes for war, whereas a feeling of security makes for peace.

A *qualitative* kind of disarmament, as proposed at Geneva in 1932, was a more promising approach. Firstly, because the abolition of particular weapons had a better chance of being agreed than any numerical scale. Secondly, because the general abolition of certain weapons at that time would have nullified the prospects of successful aggression. If tanks and bomber-aircraft had been universally abolished in 1932 as was then proposed—and nearly agreed—and a system of international inspection established as a check on their revival, there could have been no successful *Blitzkrieg* in 1939–40. For Hitler owed his initial victories mainly to those particular defence-breaking weapons. Numbers of troops counted for little in comparison. Indeed, his opponents had the superiority in that respect.

250

If the decisive weapons had once been banned, it would have been very difficult for Hitler to have developed them in secret to an adequate pitch for effectiveness—even without the check of an international inspectorate. For tanks and bombers largely depend for their effectiveness on their crews having operational practice in exercises—and such practice could hardly have been hidden.

But the value of any such agreement now on qualitative disarmament might be nullified because of the much greater chances of carrying out the necessary practice somewhere in the depths of Asiatic Russia, and still more because of the development of nuclear weapons and missile means of delivery. Evasion of any agreed system of inspection would be far easier than in Europe. There would also be much less chance of any fresh developments of a sinister kind being spotted and reported—unless complete freedom of travel was mutually agreed and established, so that alert and inquisitive visitors, such as newspaper correspondents, could fly over any area they wished in private planes or helicopters, land anywhere, and enter everywhere. That might be a better safeguard than any formal scheme of inspection that could be devised in a disarmament plan.

An awareness of what science is doing discourages optimism about the basic solidity of any disarmament agreement even if agreement could be reached. In earlier centuries the pace of development was very slow—and thus provided a reasonably firm basis for military calculations. Even so, there was abundant error, simply because official military minds were even slower to change their conceptions. But in this century the application of science to warfare produced an ever increasing acceleration of weapon development. That is now threatening to nullify even the possibility of military calculation.

I was one of the early advocates of what is called opera-

251

tional research—the application of the scientific method of inquiry to the study of warfare. In trying to apply it myself so far as I was able, I managed to be fairly successful in predicting, after World War I, the main military developments that governed World War II. Yet I feel very dubious now in attempting any predictions about a World War III, if war should break out—beyond the basic certainty that it would immediately produce chaos. And I do not feel much confidence in even the best organised system of operational research. Things are moving so fast in the weapon sphere that even the most scientific calculation becomes little better than speculation.

The technical instability of any military basis of settlement, and plan for mutual disarmament, thus becomes all too clear. Let me add that I do not disparage the psychological benefit of an attempt to reach some limiting agreement in the military field. Any mutual step that tends to relieve tension, and create even a limited check on aggressive action, is likely to be a help in averting war. It is worth taking some risks— short of fundamental risks—along these lines because of the psychological value. But it would be unwise to count on such steps too much, and wise to regard them as subsidiary.

The main hope of preserving peace lies on the higher level of grand strategy. Whereas strategy is only concerned with *winning a war*, grand strategy takes a longer view. Even in war it never loses sight of the peace that will follow and should guide the war with that aim always in view. It is no less needed in peace—not only to preserve peace, but to produce a better state of peace. It might be called the higher strategy of enlightened self-interest.

The conduct of grand strategy rests with statesmen— though soldiers ought to understand it, as servants of government. While it is primarily political—in the sense of policy—

it requires on the part of the political leaders an understanding of war, and particularly of how wars come about.

In dealing with the present problem, it would be wiser for Western statesmen, and all of us, to become adjusted to a continuation of difficulties, and tense manoeuvring, than to look for any definite settlement. Such settlements are uncommon in history, but situations change. That very changeability may in course of time solve our present problems indirectly. It has frequently done so in the past, even in the case of problems that seemed quite insoluble.

During the Middle Ages, the menace of Mahommedanism was an obsession with the Western Powers. From the eleventh to the fourteenth centuries a series of Crusading wars were waged without any lasting gains. Instead, they served to unite the Mahommedan world, and ended in an ominous westward spread of Mahommedan rule. Yet the tide then ebbed.

In the sixteenth and seventeenth centuries Christendom was split, and Western civilisation almost wrecked, by the wars of religion between the rival fanaticism of Catholicism and Protestantism. They caused much mutual devastation, brought no decisive result, and ended in no definite settlement—yet the seemingly insoluble problem gradually faded away.

In the nineteenth century, the sequel to the Anglo-Russian alliance in gaining victory over Napoleonic France was that Britain and British India spent ninety years under the cloud of war with Russia. Yet with the coming of the twentieth century the situation changed—Britain and Russia becoming allied again, along with France, their former enemy!

History should have taught us that no antagonistic line-up is fixed and final. A relaxation of tension, even though it may seem no more than temporary, offers the best chance of a changing situation—which can spell salvation from any current menace.

The study of war has taught me that almost every war was avoidable, and that the outbreak was most often produced by peace-desiring statesmen losing their heads, or their patience, and putting their opponent in a position where he could not draw back without serious loss of " face ". Clumsy efforts to forestall a feared aggression have too often provoked it—particularly where politically-inspired moves have jumped beyond strategic possibilities.

There have been too many recent examples. Chamberlain's " Guarantee " to Poland, in 1939, a sudden reversal of his policy of appeasement, had the obvious effect of combining provocation with temptation. No dictator, especially one like Hitler, could be expected to submit to such a slap in the face. At the same time the palpable impossibility of Britain giving any effective help to a country so remote as Poland tempted him to show the futility of the guarantee. Yet the captured German archives show that Hitler had not intended to deal with Poland in 1939, and that he only made up his mind to attack her *after* Chamberlain had made his unfulfillable offer of support. It acted like throwing down a gauntlet, or waving the proverbial red rag in the face of a bull. So the guarantee merely guaranteed that war would start at the time and in the circumstances most disadvantageous for the Western Powers.

Norway was another example. We now know that Hitler was very reluctant to embark on an invasion of Norway until Churchill's speeches and preparatory steps so alarmed him as to convince him that we were about to occupy that neutral country on his flank. While Churchill hailed that spread of the war as a German blunder that we had " provoked ", and by which " we are greatly advantaged ", it turned out greatly to our disadvantage and the damage of our friends.

Similarly, when the Communist invasion of South Korea was repulsed in 1950, a retaliatory advance beyond the 38th Parallel was the surest way of provoking the Chinese to intervene in the Korean conflict—after three months' hesitation on their part. It is a sad reflection on Western statesmen that they were carried away by the flush of success in regaining South Korea, and made no adequate effort to put a brake on the continuation of the advance.

The statesmen of the Western democracies should have learned two fundamental lessons from their bitter and repeated experiences since 1939. Don't try to bluff on an obviously weak hand. Do try to look at each step you plan from the other side's viewpoint—*before* you take the step.

There is a widespread feeling in the West that no " co-existence " compromise is really possible, or likely to last, with the Communist régimes of Russia and China—and that these will continue to exploit opportunities and grab more gains wherever they can. That feeling has much justification in experience, and in knowledge of totalitarian trends. But the more right it is, the more vital that Western statesmen in taking counter-measures should bear in mind a longstanding lesson of police experience—that " a burglar doesn't commit murder unless he is cornered ". It is as true of the community of nations as of any smaller one.

Another lesson of strategy, which should be a pillar of policy, is the importance of putting ourselves in the other's shoes and looking at every step from the other's standpoint *before* we take the step. To minimise the risks of precipitating war while we are developing our power of defence, we should endeavour to understand Communist-Russian mentality. That requires a realisation not only of its Marxist logic, missionary fervour, revolutionary ferment, and power urge; but also its underlying fears, its intense suspiciousness and

255

ignorance of the outer world—characteristics that have been accentuated by long isolation as well as by the governmental system. The same applies, with certain differences, to Communist-China.

Taking account of these mental conditions, and viewing the strategical situation from " the other side of the hill ", we may be better able to understand how steps, and which steps, on our part that are intended as defensive safeguards are liable to appear as designed to gain offensive springboards. The protective spread of American bases in the Middle East and Far East may, naturally, look from the other side like a ring of such springboards being pushed in close to the vital centres of Russia and China—thus producing, in reaction, a sharpened impulse to push them further away by expanding the area of Communist control.

It is evident that the rulers of Soviet Russia do not want to venture on war, for if they did they would have struck before the West began to rearm, when the going would have been easy. So the biggest risk now is that the Western Powers may say or do things likely to make the Russian Government feel that the Western Powers will take the offensive at a favourable opportunity. If the Russian Government became definitely convinced that such a stroke is certain to come, they would not be likely to wait for it.

From that point of view there is obviously more threat in multiplying America's strategic air force and long-range missiles than in the NATO effort to build up ground forces and tactical air forces for the defence of western and southern Europe. These forces could be built up to a strength sufficient to check a Russian invasion but that would be not nearly strong enough for an invasion of Russia. Thus they are plainly defensive, not offensive, in purpose—a shield rather than a sword.

An adequate shield force on the ground is a better safeguard than to depend purely on the retaliatory threat of nuclear bombing or missile bombardment. An atom-bomb is not a good policeman, fireman, or frontier-guard. It is uncertain of stopping an inroad or outbreak, while liable to be mutually fatal in ultimate effects.

But the best safeguard of all is for all of us to keep cool. Indignation and exasperation are primary risks, for such emotions are all too liable to produce a fatal explosion. Nothing can be more fatal than the feeling " it's bound to come—let's get it over ". War is not a way *out* from danger and strain. It is a way *down* into a pit—of unknown depth.

On the other hand, tension so intense as it has been during the last decade is almost bound to relax eventually if war is postponed long enough. This has happened often before in history, for situations change. They never remain static. But it is always dangerous to be too dynamic, and impatient, in trying to force the pace. A war-charged situation can only change in two ways. It is bound to become better, eventually, if war is avoided without surrender. Such logic has been confirmed by experience.

CPSIA information can be obtained
at www.ICGtesting.com
Printed in the USA
BVHW01s1359171217
503058BV00008B/72/P

9 781163 807378